CLASSIC
TEEN
STORIES

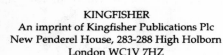

KINGFISHER
An imprint of Kingfisher Publications Plc
New Penderel House, 283-288 High Holborn
London WC1V 7HZ

This paperback edition published by Kingfisher 1999
First published in paperback by Kingfisher 1995
as *Story Library Real-Life Stories*

2 4 6 8 10 9 7 5 3 1
GROL/0203/THOM/FR/80HIB

Originally published in hardback by Kingfisher 1995
as *Story Library Growing Up Stories*

A CIP catalogue record for this
book is available from the British Library

ISBN 0 7534 0384 6

Printed in India

CLASSIC TEEN STORIES

CHOSEN BY
BETSY BYARS

ILLUSTRATED BY
ROBERT GEARY

KING*f*ISHER

CONTENTS

WHO'S AFRAID?

PHILIPPA PEARCE

"WILL MY COUSIN DICKY be there?"

"Everyone's been asked. Cousins, aunts, uncles, great-aunts, great-uncles – the lot. I've told you: it's your great-grandmother's hundredth birthday party."

"But will Dicky Hutt be there?"

"I'm sure he will be."

"Anyway, Joe, why do you want to know?"

Joe's mother and father were staring at Joe; and Joe said, "I hate Dicky."

"Now, Joe!" said his mother; and his father asked: "Why on earth do you hate Dicky?"

"I just do," said Joe. He turned away, to end the conversation; but inside his head he was saying: "I'd like to kill Dicky Hutt. Before he tries to kill me."

When the day of the birthday came, everyone – just as Joe's mother had said – was there. Relations of all ages swarmed over the little house where Great-grandmother lived, looked after by Great-aunt Madge. Fortunately, Great-grandmother had been born in the summer, and now – a hundred years later – the sun shone warmly on her celebrations. Great-aunt Madge shooed everyone into the garden for the photograph. The grown-ups sat on chairs, or stood in rows, and the children sat crossed-legged in a row in the very front. (At one end, Joe; at the other, Dicky; and Dicky's stare at Joe said: "If I catch you, I'll kill you . . .") There was a gap in the centre of this front row for a table with the tiered birthday cake and its hundred candles.

And behind the cake sat Great-grandmother in her wheel-chair, with one shawl over her knees and another round her shoulders. Great-aunt Madge stood just behind her.

Great-grandmother faced the camera with a steady gaze from eyes that saw nothing by now – she had become blind in old age. Whether she heard much was doubtful. Certainly, she never spoke or turned her head even a fraction as if to listen.

After the photograph and the cutting of the cake, the grown-ups stood around drinking tea and talking. (Great-grandmother had been wheeled off somewhere indoors for a rest.) The children, if they were very young, clung to their parents; the older ones sidled about aimlessly – aimlessly, except that Joe could see Dicky always sidling towards him, staring his hatred. So Joe sidled away and sidled away . . .

"Children!" cried Great-aunt Madge. "What about a good old game? What about hide-and-seek? There's the garden to hide in, and most of the house."

Some of the children still clung to their parents; others said "yes" to hide-and-seek. Dicky Hutt said "yes". Joe said "no"; but his father said impatiently: "Don't be soft! Go off and play with the others."

Dicky Hutt shouted: "I'll be He!" So he was. Dicky Hutt shut his eyes and began to count at once. When he had counted a hundred, he would open his eyes and begin to search.

Joe knew whom he would search for with the bitterest thoroughness: himself.

Joe was afraid – too afraid to think well. He thought at first that he would hide in the garden, where there were at least grown-ups about – but then he didn't trust Dicky not to be secretly watching under his eyelashes, to see exactly where he went. Joe couldn't bear the thought of that.

So, after all, he went indoors to hide; but by then some of the best hiding-places had been taken. And out in the garden Dicky Hutt was counting fast, shouting aloud his total at every count of ten. "Seventy!" he was shouting now; and Joe had just looked behind the sofa in the front room, and there was already someone crouching there. And there was also someone hiding under the pile of visitors' coats – "Eighty!" came Dicky Hutt's voice from the garden – and two children already in the stair-cupboard, when he thought of that hiding-place. So he must go on looking for somewhere – anywhere – to hide – and "Ninety!" from outside – *anywhere* to hide – and for the second time he came to the door with the notice pinned to it that said: "Keep out! Signed: Madge."

"A hundred! I'm coming!" shouted Dicky Hutt. And Joe turned the handle of the forbidden door and slipped inside and shut the door behind him.

The room was very dim, because the curtains had been drawn close; and its quietness seemed empty. But Joe's eyes began to be able to pick out the furnishings of the room, even in the half-light; table, chair, roll-top desk, and also – like just another piece of furniture, and just as immobile – Great-grandmother's wheelchair and Great-grandmother sitting in it.

He stood, she sat, both silent, still; and Dicky Hutt's thundering footsteps and voice were outside, passing the door, and then far away.

He thought she did not know that he had come into her room; but a low, slow voice reached him: "Who's there?"

He whispered: "It's only me – Joe."

9

Silence; and then the low, slow voice again: "Who's there?"

He was moving towards her, to speak in her very ear, when she spoke a third time: "Who's there?"

And this time he heard in her voice the little tremble of fear: he recognized it. He came to her chair, and laid his hand on hers. For a second he felt her weakly pull away, and then she let his hand rest, but turned her own, so that his hand fell into hers. She held his hand, fingered it slowly. He wanted her to know that he meant her no harm; he wanted her to say: "This is a small hand, a child's hand. You are only a child, after all."

But she did not speak again.

He stood there; she sat there; and the excited screams and laughter and running footsteps of hide-and-seek were very far away.

At last, Joe could tell from the sounds outside that the game of hide-and-seek was nearly over. He must be the last player not to be found and chased by Dicky Hutt. For now Dicky Hutt was wandering about, calling, "Come out, Joe! I know where you're hiding, Joe, so you might as well come out! I shall find you, Joe – I shall find you!"

The roving footsteps passed the forbidden doorway several times; but – no, this time they did not pass. Dicky Hutt had stopped outside.

The silence outside the door made Joe tremble: he tried to stop trembling, for the sake of the hand that held his, but he could not. He felt that old, old skin-and-bony hand close on his, as if questioning what was happening, what was wrong.

But he had no voice to explain to her. He had no voice at all.

His eyes were on the knob of the door. Even through the gloom he could see that it was turning. Then the door was creeping open – not fast, but steadily; not far, but far enough—

It opened far enough for Dicky Hutt to slip through. He

stood there, inside the dim room. Joe could see his bulk there: Dicky Hutt had always been bigger than he was; now he loomed huge. And he was staring directly at Joe.

Joe's whole body was shaking. He felt as if he were shaking to pieces. He wished that he could.

His great-grandmother held his shaking hand in hers.

Dicky Hutt took a step forward into the room.

Joe had no hope. He felt his great-grandmother lean forward a little in her chair, tautening her grip on his hand as she did so. In her low, slow voice she was saying: "Who—" And Joe thought, He won't bother to answer her; he'll just come for me. He'll *come* for me . . .

But the low, slow voice went on: "Whooooooooooooooo—" She was hooting like some ghost-throated owl; and then the hooting raised itself into a thin, eerie wailing. Next, through the wailing, she began to gibber, with effect so startling – so horrifying – that Joe forgot Dicky Hutt for a moment, and turned to look at her. His great-grandmother's mouth was partly open, and she was making her false teeth do a kind of devil's dance inside it.

And when Joe looked towards Dicky Hutt again, he had gone. The door was closing, the knob turning. The door clicked shut, and Joe could hear Dicky Hutt's feet tiptoeing away.

When Joe looked at his great-grandmother again, she was sitting back in her chair. Her mouth was closed; the gibbering and the hooting and the wailing had ceased. She looked exhausted – or had she died? But no, she was just looking unbelievably old.

He did not disturb her. He stood by her chair some time longer. Then he heard his parents calling over the house for him: they wanted to go home.

He moved his hand out of hers – the grasp was slack now: perhaps she had fallen asleep. He thought he wanted to kiss her goodbye; but then he did not want the feel of that century-old cheek against his lips.

So he simply slipped away from her and out of the room.

He never saw her again. Nearly a year later, at home, the news came of her death. Joe's mother said: "Poor old thing . . ."

Joe's father (whose grandmother Great-grandmother had been) said, "When I was a little boy, she was fun. I remember her. Jokey, then; full of tricks . . ."

Joe's mother said, "Well, she'd outlived all that. Outlived everything. Too old to be any use to herself – or to anyone else. A burden, only."

Joe said nothing; but he wished now that he had kissed her cheek, to say goodbye, and to thank her.

THE TV STAR

JUDY BLUME

from Tales of a Fourth Grade Nothing

AUNT LINDA IS MY mother's sister. She lives in Boston. Last week she had a baby girl. So now I have a new cousin. My mother decided to fly to Boston to see Aunt Linda and the new baby.

"I'll only be gone for the weekend," my mother told me.

I was sitting on her bed watching her pack. "I know," I said.

"Daddy will take care of you and Fudge."

"I know," I said again.

"Are you sure you'll be all right?" she asked me.

"Sure. Why not?"

"Will you help Daddy with Fudge?"

"Sure, Mom. Don't worry."

"I'm not worrying. It's just that Daddy is so . . . well, you know . . . he doesn't know much about taking care of children." Then she closed her suitcase.

"We'll be fine, Mom," I said. I was really looking forward to the weekend. My father doesn't care about keeping things neat. He never examines me to see if I'm clean. And he lets me stay up late at night.

On Friday morning all four of us rode down in the elevator to say goodbye to my mother.

Henry looked at the suitcase. "You going away, Mr Hatcher?" he asked.

My mother answered. "No, I am, Henry. My sister just had her first baby. I'm flying to Boston for the weekend . . . to help out."

"New baby," Fudge said. "Baby baby baby."

Nobody paid any attention to him. Sometimes my brother just talks to hear the sound of his own voice.

"Have a nice visit, Mrs Hatcher," Henry told my mother when we reached the lobby.

"Thank you, Henry," my mother said. "Keep an eye on my family for me."

"Will do, Mrs Hatcher," Henry said, giving my father a wink.

Outside my father hailed a taxi. He put the suitcase in first, then held the door for my mother. When she was settled in the cab my father said, "Don't worry about us. We'll be just fine."

"Just fine . . . just fine, Mommy," Fudge yelled.

"Bye, Mom. See you Sunday," I said.

My mother blew us kisses. Then her cab drove away.

My father sighed while Fudge jumped up and down calling, "Bye, Mommy . . . bye bye bye!"

I had no school that day. The teachers were at a special meeting. So my father said he'd take me and Fudge to the office with him.

My father's office is in a huge building made of almost all glass. It's really a busy place. You never see people just sitting quietly at desks. Everyone's always rushing around. A person could get lost in there. My father has a private office and his own secretary. Her name is Janet and she's very pretty. I especially like her hair. It's thick and black. She has the longest eyelashes I've ever seen. Once I heard my mother say, "Janet must have to get up at the crack of dawn to put on her face." My father just laughed when my mother said it.

Janet's seen me before but this was her first meeting with Fudge. I was glad his hair was finally growing back. I explained right off about his teeth. "He'll look a lot better when he's older," I said. "He knocked out his front two, but when he's six or seven he'll get new ones."

"See," Fudge said, opening his mouth. "All gone."

My father said, "Janet, the boys are going to be here for the morning. Can you amuse them while I clear up some work?"

"Certainly, Mr Hatcher," Janet said. "You go ahead into your office and I'll take the boys on a tour of the rest of the agency."

As soon as my father went into his private office Janet took out her handbag. She reached in and came up with a hairbrush, some lipstick, and a bag of crackers. "Want some?" she asked me and Fudge.

"Okay," I said, taking a handful. Fudge did the same. The crackers were shaped like little goldfish. I nibbled while Janet fixed herself up. She had a big folding mirror in her desk drawer. She set it on top of her desk and went to work on herself. When she was finished she looked exactly the same as when we came in. But I guess she didn't think so because she said, "That's much better." Then she put all her stuff away and took me by one hand and Fudge by the other.

We walked down a long hall through a doorway and into another section of the agency. We came to a room where there were a bunch of kids with mothers. I guess there were at least fifty of them. Most of the kids were kind of small, like Fudge. Some were crying.

"Is this a nursery school or what?" I asked Janet.

She laughed. "They're here to try out for the new Toddle-Bike commercial."

"You mean they all want to be the kid who rides the Toddle-Bike on TV?"

"Yes. At least their mothers want them to be picked," Janet said. "But we can only use one."

"You mean only one out of all these kids is going to be picked?"

"That's right," Janet said.

"Who picks him?" I asked.

"Your father and Mr Denberg are doing it. But of course Mr Vincent, the president of the Toddle-Bike company, has to approve."

Just then a door opened and a secretary came out. "Next," she called to the waiting kids.

"My Murray's next!" a mother said.

"Oh no he's not!" another mother called. "Sally is next."

"Ladies . . . please! You'll all have a turn," the secretary said.

Murray got to be next. He was a little redheaded kid. He wasn't in the other room for two minutes when the door opened and a big man with a cigar in his mouth came out. "No, no, no!" he shouted. "He's not the type at all."

Murray was crying. His mother yelled at the big man. "What do you know, anyway? You wouldn't know a treasure if you found one!" She shook her fist at him.

Janet whispered to me. "That's Mr Vincent, the president of Toddle-Bike."

16

Mr Vincent walked to the centre of the room. He looked around at all the kids. When he looked over at us he pointed and called. "There he is! That's the kid I want!"

I thought he meant me. I got excited. I could just see myself on TV riding the Toddle-Bike. All my friends would turn on their sets and say, "Hey, look! There's Peter."

While I was thinking about what fun it would be Mr Vincent came over to us and grabbed Fudge. He lifted him up. "Perfect!" he cried. "He's perfect."

The mothers who were waiting packed up their kids and left right away.

Mr Vincent took off with Fudge in his arms. Janet chased him. She called, "But, Mr Vincent . . . you don't understand . . ."

I ran after Janet.

Mr Vincent carried Fudge into the other room. He announced, "I found him myself! The perfect kid to ride the Toddle-Bike in my new commercial."

Mr Vincent put Fudge down and took the cigar out of his mouth. There were two other men in the room. One of them was Mr Denberg. The other one was my father.

"Hi, Daddy," Fudge said.

"George," my father told Mr Vincent, "this is my son! He's no actor or model. He can't make your Toddle-Bike commercial."

"He doesn't have to be an actor or a model. He's perfect the way he is!" Mr Vincent insisted.

"Now look, George . . . we want to make the best possible commercial for your company. But Fudge can't be the boy to ride the Toddle-Bike."

"Now you listen, Hatcher!" Mr Vincent raised his voice.

I wondered why he called my father Hatcher – just like Mr Yarby did.

Mr Vincent pointed to Fudge. "Either that kid rides my Toddle-Bike or I take my account to another advertising agency. It's that simple."

My father looked at Mr Denberg.

"It's your decision, Warren," Mr Denberg told my father. "I don't want to be the one to tell you what to do."

My father picked up Fudge and held him on his lap. "Would you like to ride the Toddle-Bike, Fudge? It's just like the one you have at home."

"Why are you asking him?" I said. "What does he know about making commercials?"

My father acted like he'd forgotten I was even around. "I'm thinking, Peter," he said. "Please be quiet."

"Well, Hatcher," Mr Vincent said. "What'll it be? This kid of yours or do I move to another agency?"

I remembered how my father lost the Juicy-O account because of Fudge. Now maybe he'd lose this one too. And I don't think he can afford that.

Finally my father said, "All right, George. You can use him . . . on one condition, though."

"What's that, Hatcher?" Mr Vincent asked.

"The commercial has to be made this afternoon. After today my son Fudge won't be available."

"That's fine with me, Hatcher," Mr Vincent said.

"Is he going to get paid?" I asked my father.

"I'll worry about that, Peter," my father said. That probably meant *yes*. He'd be paid and have lots of money in the bank. I'd have nothing. And some day I'd have to borrow from him. No – wait a minute – never! I'll never borrow money from Fudge. I'll starve first! "Can I at least watch when you make the commercial?" I asked.

"Certainly," my father said. "You can watch the whole thing."

I turned to Mr Denberg. "Will Fudge be famous?" I asked.

"No, not famous . . . but a lot of people will think he looks familiar," Mr Denberg said.

I turned to Mr Vincent. "Do you know he has no front top teeth?"

"That's part of his charm," Mr Vincent said.

"And he cut off all his hair two months ago."

"Well, he looks fine now," Mr Vincent said.

"And he can't even talk in long sentences yet," I told everyone in the room.

"He doesn't have to say a word," Mr Vincent told me.

I couldn't think of any other reason why Mr Vincent shouldn't use Fudge in his Toddle-Bike commercial. It was settled. Soon Fudge would be a famous television star and I would be plain old Peter Hatcher – fourth grade nothing.

"Let's begin right after lunch," Mr Denberg said. "We should get it filmed in about two hours."

While my father and Mr Denberg worked out all the arrangements I asked Janet where the men's room was. She walked me to it. I told her thank you and that she didn't have to wait. I'd find my own way back.

When I was safely inside I looked at myself in the mirror. *I wish Fudge had never been born*, I thought. *Everything good always happens to him! If he had to be born I wish he could be nine or ten – like me. Then Mr Vincent wouldn't want him to be the one to ride the Toddle-Bike in his commercial.*

Janet sent down to the coffee shop for some sandwiches and drinks. After we ate we all walked to another section of the agency where the cameras were set up. A make-believe street scene was the background. The Toddle-Bike was shiny red. My father told Fudge all he had to do was ride it around. Fudge liked that. He zoomed all over the place. "Vroom-vroom-vroom," he called.

My father, Mr Vincent, and Janet sat on folding chairs and watched the action. I sat on the floor, at my father's side. Mr Denberg was the director. He said, "Okay, Fudge . . . we're ready to begin now. You ride the Toddle-Bike where I tell you to and I'll take a picture of you doing it . . . all right?"

"No," Fudge said.

"What does he mean, Hatcher?" Mr Vincent asked. "Why did he say *no*?"

My father groaned. "Look, George . . . using Fudge was your idea – not mine."

Mr Denberg tried again. "Okay, Fudge . . . this is it . . ."

The cameraman said, "Start riding this way . . . ready, set, go!"

Fudge sat there on the Toddle-Bike. But he wouldn't pedal.

"Come on, kid . . . let's go!" the cameraman called.

"No. Don't want to!" Fudge answered.

"What's with this kid, Mr Hatcher?" the cameraman asked.

"Fudge," my father said, "do what the nice man tells you to."

"No! Don't have to!"

Janet whispered to my father. "How about some cookies, Mr Hatcher?"

"Good idea, Janet," my father told her.

"I have some Oreos right here," she said, patting her handbag. "Shall I give them to him?"

"One at a time," my father said.

Janet walked across the room to Fudge. He was still sitting on the Toddle-Bike. "If you do what the nice man says, you can have a cookie," Janet told him.

"Show me," Fudge said.

Janet held up a box of Oreos. *She was really well prepared*, I thought. *She must eat all day long, what with the crackers shaped like goldfish and a whole box of Oreos too.* I wondered what else she had in that handbag.

"Give me," Fudge said.

Janet held up one cookie. Fudge reached for it, but Janet didn't let him get it. "If you do what the nice man says you can have an Oreo. Maybe even two or three Oreos."

"First cookie," Fudge said.

"First do what the nice man says," Janet told him.

"No! First cookie!"

"Give him one, Janet," Mr Denberg called. "We haven't got all day to fool around."

Janet gave Fudge one Oreo. He ate it up.

"Okay, kid . . . all ready now?" the cameraman said.

20

"You ride over to me."

Fudge didn't do it.

Mr Vincent was losing his patience. "Hatcher," he hollered. "You get that son of yours to ride my Toddle-Bike or I'm taking my whole account away from you and your agency!"

"Must I remind you, George . . . using Fudge was your idea – not mine!" my father said.

"Forget about whose idea it was, Hatcher. He's your kid. You better get through to him . . . now!"

"I have an idea," my father said. He walked to a corner of the room and beckoned to the others. Mr Denberg and Mr Vincent gathered around him, along with the cameraman and Janet. They looked like a bunch of football players huddled together talking about the next play.

Soon my father called me. "Peter . . . would you join us, please?"

"Sure, Dad," I said. "What is it?"

"Peter . . . we want you to ride the Toddle-Bike for us. To show Fudge how it's done."

"But he already knows how to ride," I said. "Didn't you see him zooming around?"

"He won't do it for the cameras, though," my father explained. "So we need your help."

"Will I be in the commercial too?" I asked.

"Well, the Toddle-Bike is really for very young children," Mr Denberg said. "Otherwise we'd have you do it in a minute."

I got the message. It was like buying the shoes and like at Dr Brown's office. They were going to use me to get Fudge to do what they wanted him to. I wondered how anybody would ever manage my brother without my help.

I walked over to Fudge and told him I was going to ride the Toddle-Bike. "Get off," I said.

Fudge held on to the bike. "No . . . mine!"

"It's not yours," my father told him.

But Fudge wouldn't move for anything. He closed his eyes and screamed. Can he scream loud when he tries!

So my father had to pull him off the Toddle-Bike. Fudge kicked and kept screaming and I'll bet Mr Vincent was sorry that he ever spotted my brother in the first place.

I got on the Toddle-Bike. It was so small my knees practically touched the ground. But I managed to ride it around just where the cameraman told me to.

"See how nice Peter can ride the Toddle-Bike," Janet said. "Here, Peter . . . come have an Oreo. You did that so well you can have two or three if you want."

Fudge stopped screaming. "ME!" he said.

"What?" my father asked him.

"Me . . . ride . . . me!"

"You can't ride as well as Peter can," Mr Denberg said.

"Can so," Fudge told him.

"I don't think so," Mr Denberg said. "You already had a turn. You didn't do what I told you to do."

"ME!"

"You want to try again?" my father asked.

"Again," Fudge said. "Again again again."

"Well . . . I don't know," Mr Denberg said.

"Well . . ." Mr Vincent said, chewing on his cigar.

"Well . . ." the cameraman said, scratching his head.

"Please!" Fudge begged.

I never heard my brother say *please* before.

Mr Denberg said, "Okay . . . we'll give you one more chance."

Fudge ran to the Toddle-Bike. I got off and he jumped on. "Now?" he asked Mr Denberg.

"Now," Mr Denberg said. "Ride this way, Fudge . . . over here . . . towards me."

Fudge did as he was told. "Just like Pee-tah!" he said. "See . . . just like Pee-tah!"

Janet gave me a kiss on my cheek. "You saved the day, Peter Hatcher!" she said.

When she wasn't looking I wiped my face. Her kiss was too juicy.

BILGEWATER

JANE GARDAM

Marigold's father is a House Master at a boy's boarding school.

WHAT ALL THIS RIGMAROLE is meant to lead up to is the fact that although I had spent, quaintly and princess-like, so much of my life among people years and years older than myself and knew something about the peculiarities of grown-ups, I knew absolutely nothing about myself and others of my age, and this is what made the first revelations, when they came, so unnerving.

There were two of these in particular and they were several years apart, not dramatic or exciting to anybody else, but a swarm of troubles and misconceptions and shynesses and agonies sprang out of them.

Both of them were to do with the boy Terrapin.

The first was when I was thirteen and I was sitting in my bedroom towards the end of summer quite late one evening. It was still light – one of the occasional northern summer nights when it doesn't ever get completely dark at all and you remember that Norway is only a few hundred miles away, nearer than Cornwall. It was a night as warm

as Cornwall, light, shadowy, soft, not heavy or thundery; a
basking, sleepy, scented night that makes you sigh and
slowly blink and gaze.

My bedroom window is a big one, low, with a sash, and
I had been lying on my stomach doing my homework.

I had finished this now, and by lying with my elbows
supporting my hands, which were under my chin, my
nose rested on the bottom of the sill. Thus above the sill
were only my great glasses and my luminous and
disgusting orange hair.

I am very long-sighted. I took my glasses off and gazed
across the evening. There stood our garden first, pretty as
a fire screen, a lovely, hazy embroidered mixture of holly-
hocks, tobacco plants and roses all tangled up together
against an old brick wall. Beyond the garden was the
kitchen garden of the House with the Fives Court at the
end of it, surrounded by tall trees, and then, to my eyes
more clear than all the rest, was the distant high line of
moors drawn with a sharp point across a great gentle sky.
There were late sounds from the Fives Court, plonk, ker-
plonk, thud, bump, and yells of boys' voices. Somewhere
about I could hear a boy practising on a flute. One, two,
three notes, pause. Yell, ker-plonk, "Oh blast you, Jenks."
One-two-three-four pause. Twitter of birds. The evening
breeze, Ker-plonk. Onetwo-threefour (go on, well done)
fivesix, came the notes, then down again. Pause – then the
whole phrase, effortless this time, complete. Mozart.
Wonderful.

I was utterly content with the content of being in the
right place at the right time. I, Marigold Green, a figure
properly set in a picture, an equation on a page, a note in a
bit of music, non-transposable, irreplaceable. Ugly, quaint
and square lay I, happy and at home where I belonged.
Sleepily and happily I watched the boy with the flute – it
was nice, ordinary Boakes – walk mazily through the
lettuces, beneath me across the lawn.

"BILGEWATER!"

I jumped so my chin cracked down on the window ledge. I swivelled my eyes, grabbed my glasses and stuck them onto my face.

"FILTHY BILGEWATER!"

I turned my face and saw the boy Terrapin hanging out of a window. He was twelve then, a new boy, but he had made himself felt from the moment he had arrived last September. Even though he was quite close – the dormitory sticking out at right angles from the Private Side and looking down at our garden, too – I couldn't mistake him. He had a voice, prematurely breaking, like a rookery.

"BILGEWATER! FILTHY BILGEWATER! WATCHING US UNDRESSING!"

Then I noticed that there were other boys behind him inside the open windows, springing about, getting ready for bed. Terrapin I saw had no clothes on his top half, and his bottom half was hidden by the window. Behind him I could see a leaping figure now and then, very white and dazzling, swinging pairs of pyjama trousers round its head.

"BILGEWATER'S GOT A FILTHY MIND," sang Terrapin.

A hand came out of a window over his head, got down into his hair and jerked him back out of sight and the dormitory monitor – Jack Rose, a year older than me – looked out quickly, rather embarrassedly, saw me, gave me a curt nod and vanished.

Jack Rose was the nicest boy in the school. There's always one, says Paula. Silver-spoon boys, she calls them – good-looking, good at games, good at work and charming. Intending to be a doctor. They're always going to be doctors, Paula says. Once when he had seen me coming along home from school, he had tweaked my hair as if it wasn't vile and said, "Hello, Marigold" (not Bilgewater) and I had dropped my satchel with the ecstasy of it all. A great huge heap of homework I'd been carrying had gone shooting over the pavement and he had helped pick it up and walked back home with me. He had pulled a funny

face but not derisive at the door of the Private Side and winked. I cared more for Jack Rose's good opinion than for rubies and the sound of trumpets.

And now he believed – what did he believe? He believed I was – what did he think? He thought I was a – (I began to blush scarlet) – a Peeping Tom! With the full horror of it, I began to sink down onto the floor two feet beneath the sill and to press my face into the linoleum, rolling my cheeks against it, then into the smooth surface of my homework book. Perhaps I *am*, I thought. Perhaps I *am* a Peeping Tom. I began to weep. I asked to die.

I decided that if ever I have a daughter like me, which heaven forbid, I shall be available on an occasion like this. I shan't be taking Private Coaching like Father or out playing wild and passionate tennis like Paula. I shall be there.

"Darling – whatever's the matter? Why ever are you crying?"

"Oh, oh, he said I was a Peeping Tom."

"Don't be ridiculous, Marigold. Who said you were a Peeping Tom? What rubbish!" and my sweet mother's head shoots from the window. Glare, glare of her eyes towards the dormitories. "You boys be quiet and go to bed at once." Down comes the window.

"Marigold, darling, don't cry. Don't be silly. Who said—?"

"Terrapin said."

"Terrapin! You goose, you goose, you beautiful goose! (My, what a wallow!) Will you please sit up and blow your nose and tell me when ever anybody listened to Terrapin?"

"Never." (Gulp. Sob).

"Well, then—"

"He said—"

"As if anyone would ever peep at Terrapin! At Terrapin!"

Watery smile.

"They'd turn to stone. Like the Gorgon's head."

(Giggle. Laugh.)

Incident over. Terrapin ever after called the Gorgon's Head and my mother and I laughing about it as the years roll by. "D'you remember that night when Terrapin called you a Peeping Tom?"

"That's what will happen to *my* daughter," I thought. "I'll see to that." Down on the floor I lay upon my silky exercise book for hours. After the first hour I thought, "I shall continue to lie here for ever. I shall lie here all night and I may die. No one will come." I wetted the exercise book with tears. I felt the tears trickle down my nose side and onto the page, and the ink spread, turning my ugly writing to a fuzz.

"I will lie here till morning."

But after what seemed to be the best part of the night, in a daze I gave the most colossal sigh and heaved myself up and stretched up to shut the window. The Boys' Dormitory windows were still wide open but dark. The Fives Court was silent. In the glimmering shadowy night I heard steps below me and saw Paula and Father coming slowly through the garden, Paula still in tennis clothes white among the flowers now faded into white as well. Father's voice was quiet and unperturbed and Paula laughed her loud, nice laugh. They walked easily along together, Paula swinging her tennis racket about, and passed out of sight. I felt a great yearning towards something or other, but slammed down my window as noisily as possible and went to bed in all my clothes.

The second incident was on a lovely day, too – in the summer holidays, with the House empty except for us, the big front door wide open and the sunshine pouring in. Paula was out in the raspberries. I'd asked her if she'd wanted help, but she had wanted to be by herself. She sings when she's by herself, very loud and rather off-key. She knows this bothers me, try as I may not to show it. So often she goes off by herself and has a good sing when there's no one about.

If you remember, I mentioned the swimming pool and how precious it is to me in the school holidays and how Father would suddenly appear beside it as I was swimming and look at me simultaneously with Aeschylus, and, Aeschylus winning, would wander away.

This day – the summer after the Peeping Tom affair – I had decked myself in a Japanese dressing gown I had found in one of Paula's clothes boxes. Goodness knows where it had come from, but it's as well that it was there because I had been setting off down the main stairs in just my bathing dress and I am square and thick; but something made me turn back and have a burrow about. I took off my glasses and put on a pair of queer old pink high-heeled shoes with pink feathers growing out of them on my bare feet, grabbed a towel and set off. In the hall sat Boakes, reading, outside Father's study door, so I was much relieved I had. As I passed, I suppose he saw the feathers go by and looked up and said, "Hello. You swimming? Want to go for a walk?" I said, "No, thank you, Boakes," because it wouldn't be very thrilling since he would have read all the time with the end of his nose grazing the paper, and I sailed ahead to the pool. I swam about for a while and soon there was Father, who must have got rid of Boakes after setting him to the gate. After a few more lengths I looked up again to see that, as usual, he had disappeared, but that Terrapin had taken his place.

Terrapin was a local boy but a boarder. There are many fewer boarders as Father's school than day boys and there is a long list of boys waiting to be boarders. Nowadays boarders, says Paula, all seem to come from broken homes or are in need of care and protection or are characters of exceptional depravity. You have to be pretty deserving to get in as a boarder from a distance, so you can imagine what sort of a hard case you have to be to get in as a boarder when you live just a few miles away, as Terrapin did.

Great rumours circulated about Terrapin – both parents were said to have put their heads in gas ovens, all his other relatives were alleged to have gone to Australia in a body rather than take him on. One somehow heard these things – half heard them from gossip among girls at the Comprehensive and what seeped into my ears around Father's House, though never a breath did I hear from Father or Paula, who never even hinted to anyone that they knew the slightest thing about any boy's private life.

But there was clearly something spectacularly odd about Terrapin because not only was he a boarder and local but now it appeared we'd got him in the school holidays, too. There Terrapin stood in Father's place at the edge of the pool.

"Hi, Bilgewater," he said.

He had a sepulchral voice now, still hoarse and rough as when breaking. Terrapin's voice was taking its time, breaking slowly, like the dawn on a wet day. But it was a voice of great power and when he spoke his eyes stuck out and cords appeared in his neck. He grunted at intervals between statements, and simultaneously with the grunts he picked his nose. He was a very short boy with fine, straight, white-yellow hair which came from a central point

on his skull and hung down all around with his awful face peering out of the middle. He looked like a small albino ape.

I said, "Get out," and turned on my back. Then, thinking of his sticking-out eyes scanning my big hips, I turned on my front again.

"Where's your father?" He was looking at me, and not at my face either, with a really frightful leer, and I began to kick my feet up and down tremendously, sending up a wake like a battleship. I rushed down the pool at a rate of knots.

When I got to the steps at the other end, he was there, squatting down at the top of them, waiting for me to come up, so I spread myself out underneath him with my arms and elbows lying along the railing round the edge, and I stared into the distance.

I heard grunt, grunt up above.

He said, "You haven't half got nice arms."

I kicked off and did a thundering sprint down the pool again with my head in the water all the way, only my legs moving, with water going up fit to raise rainbows. When I got to the far end, I kept my back to him and hung on to the hand rail. When eventually I got out, he had gone.

I felt sick. He was the most revolting thing I had ever seen. He was like Caliban – Paula had been reading me *The Tempest* on Thursdays. He was so foul I should have liked to get him by his beastly ankles and drag him into the water and trample him down. Every time he came up for air, all snotty, neck and eyes bulging, down I would bash him.

"Bilge! Bilgewater! Help! Help!"

"*Down* you go, you filthy boy."

"Help! Help! I can't swim!"

"Drown, then!"

But the terrible thing at the time (I think I was thirteen. I might just have been fourteen. Perhaps I was twelve) – the unthinkable thing was that when he said that about my arms I felt pins and needles sweep over me in a wave, starting at the top of my skull, rushing downwards to the base of my spine.

"You haven't half got nice arms."

I examined my arms that night at bedtime, turning them outwards and inwards. I have a pale skin and a very precise blue vein going diagonally across the inside of the elbow. The hands at the ends of the arms are all right, too, with pointed, effective fingers and clean nails. I like clean nails.

Mrs Gathering, the Headmaster's wife at Father's school, once came to tea when I was small. She brought her daughter – the one I rather got on with, the one who went away. Funnily enough, I can't remember the daughter on that occasion, though I think there was something about her breaking one of my dolls. All I remember is Mrs Gathering getting hold of one of my hands by the tea trolley and saying, "Beautiful hands." She said it dramatically. I thought she was a bit of an ass. But I remembered the compliment – my first. This one of Terrapin's was my second.

My hands and my arms. My hands and my arms. I asked Paula next day if I could have a sleeveless dress and she said, "Yes, my duck. If ever I get the toime."

THE DAY IT RAINED
COCKROACHES

PAUL ZINDEL

from The Pigman and Me

THE THREE OF US were very excited when we pulled up in front of our new home. There were some unusual things about it, but I've always been attracted to unusual things. For instance, I was the only kid I knew who always liked searching newspapers to find weird news. Whenever I found a shocking article or picture, I'd save it. That week alone, I had cut out a picture of a man who was born with monkey feet, a list of Seventy-Five Ways to Be Richer a Year from Now, and a report about a mother who sold her daughter to Gypsies in exchange for a theatre trip to London. Also, there are ten biographical points about me you should know right off the bat:

1) My father ran away with one of his girlfriends when I was two years old.
2) My sister taught me how to cut out fake coins from

34

cardboard and make imitation lamb chops out of clay, because we never had very much real money or food.

3) I once wanted to be Batman and fly off buildings.

4) I yearned to be kidnapped by aliens for a ride in their flying saucer.

5) Ever since I could remember I'd liked to make cyclorama displays out of shoeboxes and cut out figures of ghosts, beasts, and teenagers to put in them.

6) I once prayed to own a pet gorilla.

7) I used to like to play tricks on people, like putting thumbtacks on their seats.

8) When my father's father was sixteen, he got a job on a Dutch freighter, sailed to America, jumped ship and swam to Staten Island, got married, and opened a bake shop, and he and his wife died from eating too many crumbcakes before Betty and I could meet them.

9) A truck once ran over my left elbow. It really hurt and left a little scar.

10) I am afraid I will one day die by shark attack.

About anything else you'd ever want to know about my preteen existence you can see in the photos in this book. However, I don't think life *really* started for me until I became a teenager and my mother moved us to Travis, on Staten Island.

When we first drove into the town, I noticed a lot of plain wood houses, a Catholic church, a war memorial, three saloons with men sitting outside on chairs, seventeen women wearing kerchiefs on their heads, a one-engine firehouse, a big red-brick school, a candy store, and a butcher shop with about 300 sausages hanging in the window. Betty shot me a private look, signalling she was aghast. Travis was mainly a Polish town, and was so special-looking that, years later, it was picked as a location for filming the movie *Splendour in the Grass*, which starred Natalie Wood (before she drowned), and Warren Beatty (before he dated Madonna). Travis was selected because they needed a town that looked like it was Kansas in 1920, which it still looks like.

The address of our new home was 123 Glen Street. We stopped in front, and for a few moments the house looked normal: brown shingles, pea-soup-green-painted sides, a tiny yellow porch, untrimmed hedges, and a rickety wood gate and fence. Across the street to the left was a slope with worn gravestones all over it. The best-preserved ones were at the top, peeking out of patches of poison oak.

The backyard of our house was an airport. I mean, the house had two acres of land of its own, but beyond the rear fence was a huge field consisting of a single dirt runway, lots of old propeller-driven Piper Cub-type planes, and a cluster of rusted hangars. This was the most underprivileged airport I'd ever seen, bordered on its west side by the Arthur Kill channel and on its south side by a Con Edison electric power plant with big black mountains of coal. The only great sight was a huge apple tree on the far left corner of our property. Its trunk was at least three feet wide. It had strong, thick branches rich with new, flapping leaves. It reached upwards like a giant's hand grabbing for the sky.

"Isn't everything beautiful?" Mother beamed.

"Yes, Mom," I said.

Betty gave me a pinch for lying.

"I'll plant my own rose garden," Mother went on, fumbling for the key. "Lilies, tulips, violets!"

Mom opened the front door and we went inside. We were so excited, we ran through the echoing empty rooms, pulling up old, soiled shades to let the sunlight crash in. We ran upstairs and downstairs, all over the place like wild ponies. The only unpleasant thing, from my point of view, was that we weren't the only ones running around. There were a lot of cockroaches scurrying from our invading footfalls and the shafts of light.

"Yes, the house has a few roaches," Mother confessed. "We'll get rid of them in no time!"

"How?" Betty asked raising an eyebrow.

"I bought eight Gulf Insect Bombs!"

"Where are they?" I asked.

Mother dashed out to the car and came back with one of the suitcases. From it she spilled the bombs, which looked like big silver hand grenades.

"We just put one in each room and turn them on!" Mother explained.

She took one of the bombs, set it in the middle of the upstairs kitchen, and turned on its nozzle. A cloud of gas began to stream from it, and we hurried into the other rooms to set off the other bombs.

"There!" Mother said. "Now we have to get out!"

"Get out?" I coughed.

"Yes. We must let the poison fill the house for four hours before we can come back in! Lucky for us there's a Lassie double feature playing at the Ritz!"

We hadn't been in the house ten minutes before we were driving off again!

I suppose you might as well know now that my mother really *loved* Lassie movies. The only thing she enjoyed more were movies in which romantic couples got killed at the end by tidal waves, volcanoes, or other natural disasters. Anyway, I was glad we were gassing the

roaches, because they are the one insect I despise. Tarantulas I like. Scorpions I can live with. But ever since I was three years old and my mother took me to a World's Fair, I have had nightmares about cockroaches. Most people remember an exciting water ride this fair had called the Shoot-the-Chutes, but emblazoned on my brain is the display the fair featured of giant, live African cockroaches, which look like American cockroaches except they're six inches long, have furry legs, and can pinch flesh. In my nightmares about them, I'm usually lying on a bed in a dark room and I notice a bevy of giant cockroaches heading for me. I try to run away but find out that someone has secretly tied me down on the bed, and the African roaches start crawling up the sides of the sheets. They walk all over my body, and then they head for my face. When they start trying to drink from my mouth is when I wake up screaming.

So after the movie I was actually looking forward to going back to the house and seeing all the dead cockroaches.

"Wasn't Lassie wonderful?" Mother sighed as she drove us back to Travis. "The way that brave dog was able to crawl hundreds of miles home after being kidnapped and beaten by Nazi Secret Service Police!"

"Yes, Mom," I agreed, although I was truthfully tired of seeing a dog movie star keep pulling the same set of tear-jerking stunts in each of its movies.

"Maybe we'll get a dog just like Lassie one day," Mother sighed.

When we got back to the house this time, we didn't run into it. We walked inside very slowly, sniffing for the deadly gas. I didn't care about the gas so much as I wanted to see a lot of roach corpses all over the place so I'd be able to sleep in peace.

But there were none.

"Where are all the dead roaches?" I asked.

"I don't know," Mother admitted.

We crept slowly upstairs to see if the bodies might be there. I knew the kitchen had the most roaches, but when we went in, I didn't see a single one, living or dead. The lone empty Gulf Insect Bomb sat spent in the middle of the floor. My sister picked up the bomb and started reading the directions. One thing my mother never did was follow directions. As Betty was reading, I noticed a closed closet door and reached out to turn its knob.

"It says here we should've opened all the closet doors before setting off the bombs, so roaches can't hide." Betty moaned, her clue to me that Mom had messed up again.

I had already started to open the door. My mind knew what was going to happen, but it was too late to tell my hand to stop pulling on the door. It sprang open, and suddenly, 5,000 very angry, living cockroaches rained down on me from the ceiling of the closet.

"Eeehhhhhh!" I screamed, leaping around the room, bathed in bugs, slapping at the roaches crawling all over me and down my neck! "Eeehhhhhh! Eeehh! Ehhh! Ehh!"

"Don't worry. I'll get more bombs," Mother said comfortingly as she grabbed an old dishrag to knock the fluttering roaches off my back. Betty calmly reached out her foot to crunch as many as dared run by her.

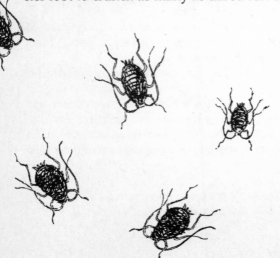

THE DOLL'S HOUSE

KATHERINE MANSFIELD

WHEN DEAR OLD MRS HAY went back to town after staying with the Burnells she sent the children a doll's house.

It was so big that the carter and Pat carried it into the courtyard, and there it stayed, propped up on two wooden boxes beside the feed-room door. No harm could come to it; it was summer. And perhaps the smell of paint would have gone off by the time it had to be taken in. For, really, the smell of paint coming from that doll's house ("Sweet of old Mrs Hay of course; most sweet and generous!") – but the smell of paint was quite enough to make anyone seriously ill, in Aunt Beryl's opinion. Even before the sacking was taken off. And when it was . . .

There stood the doll's house, a dark, oily, spinach green, picked out with bright yellow. Its two solid little chimneys, glued on to the roof, were painted red and white, and the door, gleaming with yellow varnish, was like a little slab of toffee. Four windows, real windows, were divided into panes by a broad streak of green. There was actually a tiny porch, too, painted yellow, with big lumps of congealed paint hanging along the edge.

But perfect, perfect little house! Who could possibly mind the smell. It was part of the joy, part of the newness.

"Open it quickly, someone!"

The hook at the side was stuck fast. Pat prised it open with his penknife, and the whole house front swung back, and – there you were, gazing at one and the same moment into the drawing-room and dining-room, the kitchen and two bedrooms. That is the way for a house to open! Why don't all houses open like that? How much more exciting than peering through the slit of a door into a mean little hall with a hat-stand and two umbrellas! That is – isn't it? – what you long to know about a house when you put your hand on the knocker. Perhaps it is the way God opens houses at the dead of night when He is taking a quiet turn with an angel . . .

"Oh-oh!" The Burnell children sounded as though they were in despair. It was too marvellous; it was too much for them. They had never seen anything like it in their lives. All the rooms were papered. There were pictures on the walls, painted on the paper, with gold frames complete. Red carpet covered all the floors except the kitchen; red plush chairs in the drawing-room, green in the dining-room; tables, beds with real bed-clothes, a cradle, a stove, a dresser with tiny plates and one big jug. But what Kezia liked more than anything, what she liked frightfully, was the lamp. It stood in the middle of the dining-room table, an exquisite little amber lamp with a white globe. It was even filled all ready for lighting, though, of course, you couldn't light it. But there was something inside that looked like oil and moved when you shook it.

The father and mother dolls, who sprawled very stiff as though they had fainted in the drawing-room, and their two little children asleep upstairs, were really too big for the doll's house. They didn't look as though they belonged. But the lamp was perfect. It seemed to smile at Kezia, to say, "I live here." The lamp was real.

The Burnell children could hardly walk to school fast enough the next morning. They burned to tell everybody,

to describe, to – well – to boast about their doll's house before the school-bell rang.

"I'm to tell," said Isabel, "because I'm the eldest. And you two can join in after. But I'm to tell first."

There was nothing to answer. Isabel was bossy, but she was always right, and Lottie and Kezia knew too well the powers that went with being eldest. They brushed through the thick buttercups at the road edge and said nothing.

"And I'm to choose who's to come and see it first. Mother said I might."

For it had been arranged that while the doll's house stood in the courtyard they might ask the girls at school, two at a time, to come and look. Not to stay to tea, of course, or to come traipsing through the house. But just to stand quietly in the courtyard while Isabel pointed out the beauties, and Lottie and Kezia looked pleased . . .

But hurry as they might, by the time they had reached the tarred palings of the boy's playground the bell had begun to jangle. They only just had time to whip off their hats and fall into line before the roll was called. Never mind. Isabel tried to make up for it by looking very important and mysterious and by whispering behind her hand to the girls near her, "Got something to tell you at playtime."

Playtime came and Isabel was surrounded. The girls of her class nearly fought to put their arms around her, to walk away with her, to beam flatteringly, to be her special friend. She held quite a court under the huge pine trees at the side of the playground. Nudging, giggling together, the little girls pressed up close. And the only two who stayed outside the ring were the two who were always outside, the little Kelveys. They knew better than to come anywhere near the Burnells.

For the fact was, the school the Burnell children went to was not at all the kind of place their parents would have chosen if there had been any choice. But there was none. It was the only school for miles. And the consequence was all the children of the neighbourhood, the Judge's little girls, the doctor's daughters, the store-keeper's children, the milk-man's, were forced to mix together. Not to speak of there being an equal number of rude, rough little boys as well. But the line had to be drawn somewhere. It was drawn at the Kelveys. Many of the children, including the Burnells, were not allowed even to speak to them. They walked past the Kelveys with their heads in the air, and as they set the fashion in all matters of behaviour, the Kelveys were shunned by everybody. Even the teacher had a special voice for them, and a special smile for the other children when Lil Kelvey came up to her desk with a bunch of dreadfully common-looking flowers.

They were the daughters of a spry, hard-working little washerwoman, who went about from house to house by the day. This was awful enough. But where was Mr Kelvey? Nobody knew for certain. But everybody said he was in prison. So they were the daughters of a washerwoman and a gaolbird. Very nice company for other people's children! And they looked it. Why Mrs Kelvey made them so conspicuous was hard to understand. The truth was they were dressed in "bits" given to her by the people for whom she worked. Lil, for instance, was a stout, plain child, with big freckles, came to school in a dress made from a green art-serge tablecloth of the Burnells', with red plush sleeves from the Logan's curtains. Her hat, perched on top of her high forehead, was a grown-up woman's hat, once the property of Miss Lecky, the postmistress. It was turned up at the back and trimmed with a large scarlet quill. What a little guy she looked! It was impossible not to laugh. And her little sister, our Else, wore a long white dress, rather like a nightgown, and a pair of little boy's boots. But whatever our Else wore she would have looked strange. She was a tiny wishbone of a child, with cropped hair and enormous solemn eyes – a little white owl. Nobody had ever seen her smile; she scarcely ever spoke. She went through life holding on to

Lil, with a piece of Lil's skirt screwed up in her hand.
Where Lil went, our Else followed. In the playground, on
the road going to and from school, there was Lil marching
in front and our Else holding on behind. Only when she
wanted anything, or when she was out of breath, our Else
gave Lil a tug, a twitch, and Lil stopped and turned round.
The Kelveys never failed to understand each other.

Now they hovered at the edge; you couldn't stop them
listening. When the little girls turned round and sneered,
Lil, as usual, gave her silly, shamefaced smile, but our Else
only looked.

And Isabel's voice, so very proud, went on telling. The carpet made a great sensation, but so did the beds with real bedclothes, and the stove with an oven door.

When she finished Kezia broke in. "You've forgotten the lamp, Isabel."

"Oh yes," said Isabel, "and there's a teeny little lamp, all made of yellow glass, with a white globe that stands on the dining-room table. You couldn't tell it from a real one."

"The lamp's best of all," cried Kezia. She thought Isabel wasn't making half enough of the little lamp. But nobody paid any attention. Isabel was choosing the two who were to come back with them that afternoon and see it. She chose Emmie Cole and Lena Logan. But when the others knew they were all to have a chance, they couldn't be nice enough to Isabel. One by one they put their arms round Isabel's waist and walked her off. They had something to whisper to her, a secret. "Isabel's *my* friend."

Only the little Kelveys moved away forgotten; there was nothing more for them to hear.

Days passed, and as more children saw the doll's house, the fame of it spread. It became the one subject, the rage. The one question was, "Have you seen Burnells' doll's house? Oh, ain't it lovely!" "Haven't you seen it? Oh, I say!"

Even the dinner hour was given up to talking about it. The little girls sat under the pines eating their thick mutton sandwiches and big slabs of johnny cake spread with butter. While always, as near as they could get, sat the Kelveys, our Else holding on to Lil, listening too, while they chewed their jam sandwiches out of a newspaper soaked with large red blobs.

"Mother," said Kezia, "can't I ask the Kelveys just once?"

"Certainly not, Kezia."

"But why not?"

"Run away, Kezia; you know quite well why not."

At last everybody had seen it except them. On that day the subject rather flagged. It was the dinner hour. The children stood together under the pine trees, and suddenly, as they looked at the Kelveys eating out of their paper, always by themselves, always listening, they wanted to be horrid to them. Emmie Cole started the whisper.

"Lil Kelvey's going to be a servant when she grows up."

"O-oh, how awful!" said Isabel Burnell, and she made eyes at Emmie.

Emmie swallowed in a very meaning way and nodded to Isabel as she'd seen her mother do on those occasions.

"It's true – it's true – it's true," she said.

Then Lena Logan's little eyes snapped. "Shall I ask her?" she whispered.

"Bet you don't," said Jessie May.

"Pooh, I'm not frightened," said Lena. Suddenly she gave a little squeal and danced in front of the other girls. "Watch! Watch me! Watch me now!" said Lena. And sliding, gliding, dragging one foot, giggling behind her hand, Lena went over to the Kelveys.

Lil looked up from her dinner. She wrapped the rest quickly away. Our Else stopped chewing. What was coming now?

"Is it true you're going to be a servant when you grow up, Lil Kelvey?" shrilled Lena.

Dead silence. But instead of answering, Lil only gave her silly, shamefaced smile. She didn't seem to mind the question at all. What a sell for Lena! The girls began to titter.

Lena couldn't stand that. She put her hands on her hips; she shot forward. "Yah, yer father's in prison!" she hissed spitefully.

This was such a marvellous thing to have said that the little girls rushed away in a body, deeply, deeply excited, wild with joy. Someone found a long rope, and they began skipping. And never did they skip so high, run in and out so fast, or do such daring things as on that morning.

In the afternoon Pat called for the Burnell children with the buggy and they drove home. There were visitors. Isabel and Lottie, who liked visitors, went upstairs to change their pinafores. But Kezia thieved out at the back. Nobody was about; she began to swing on the big white gates of the courtyard. Presently, looking along the road, she saw two little dots. They grew bigger, they were coming towards her. Now she could see that one was in front and one close behind. Now she could see that they were the Kelveys. Kezia stopped swinging. She slipped off the gate as if she was going to run away. Then she hesitated. The Kelveys came nearer, and beside them walked their shadows, very long, stretching right across the road with their heads in the buttercups. Kezia clambered back on the gate; she had made up her mind; she swung out.

"Hullo," she said to the passing Kelveys.

They were so astounded that they stopped. Lil gave her silly smile. Our Else stared.

"You can come and see our doll's house if you want to," said Kezia, and she dragged one toe on the ground. But at that Lil turned red and shook her head quickly.

"Why not?" asked Kezia.

Lil gasped, then she said, "Your ma told our ma you wasn't to speak to us."

"Oh, well," said Kezia. She didn't know what to reply. "It doesn't matter. You can come and see our doll's house all the same. Come on. Nobody's looking."

But Lil shook her head still harder.

"Don't you want to?" asked Kezia.

Suddenly there was a twitch, a tug at Lil's skirt. She turned round. Our Else was looking at her with big, imploring eyes; she was frowning; she wanted to go. For a moment Lil looked at our Else very doubtfully. But then our Else twitched her skirt again. She started forward. Kezia led the way. Like two little stray cats they followed across the courtyard to where the doll's house stood.

"There it is," said Kezia.

There was a pause. Lil breathed loudly, almost snorted; our Else was still as stone.

"I'll open it for you," said Kezia kindly. She undid the hook and they looked inside.

"There's the drawing-room and the dining-room, and that's the –"

"Kezia!"

Oh, what a start they gave!

"Kezia!"

It was Aunt Beryl's voice. They turned round. At the back door stood Aunt Beryl, staring as if she couldn't believe what she saw.

"How dare you ask the little Kelveys into the courtyard!"

said her cold, furious voice. "You know as well as I do, you're not allowed to talk to them. Run away, children, run away at once. And don't come back again," said Aunt Beryl. And she stepped into the yard and shooed them out as if they were chickens.

"Off you go immediately!" she called, cold and proud.

They did not need telling twice. Burning with shame, shrinking together, Lil huddling along like her mother, our Else dazed, somehow they crossed the big courtyard and squeezed through the white gate.

"Wicked, disobedient little girl!" said Aunt Beryl bitterly to Kezia, and she slammed the doll's house to.

The afternoon had been awful. A letter had come from Willie Brent, a terrifying, threatening letter, saying if she did not meet him that evening in Pulman's Bush, he'd come to the front door and ask the reason why! But now

that she had frightened those little rats of Kelveys and given Kezia a good scolding, her heart felt lighter. That ghastly pressure was gone. She went back to the house humming.

When the Kelveys were well out of sight of Burnells', they sat down to rest on a big red drainpipe by the side of the road. Lil's cheeks were still burning; she took off the hat with the quill and held it on her knee. Dreamily they looked over the hay paddocks, past the creek, to the group of wattles where Logan's cows stood waiting to be milked. What were their thoughts?

Presently our Else nudged up close to her sister. But now she had forgotten the cross lady. She put out a finger and stroked her sister's quill; she smiled her rare smile.

"I seen the little lamp," she said softly.

Then both were silent once more.

THE SECRET DIARY OF
ADRIAN MOLE, AGED 13¾

SUE TOWNSEND

THURSDAY JANUARY 1ST
BANK HOLIDAY IN ENGLAND,
IRELAND, SCOTLAND AND WALES

These are my New Year's resolutions:

1. I will help the blind across the road.
2. I will hang my trousers up.
3. I will put the sleeves back on my records.
4. I will not start smoking.
5. I will stop squeezing my spots.
6. I will be kind to the dog.
7. I will help the poor and ignorant.
8. After hearing the disgusting noises from downstairs last night, I have also vowed never to drink alcohol.

My father got the dog drunk on cherry brandy at the party last night. If the RSPCA hear about it he could get done. Eight days have gone by since Christmas Day but my mother still hasn't worn the green lurex apron I bought her for Christmas! She will get bathcubes next year.

Just my luck, I've got a spot on my chin for the first day of the New Year!

Friday January 2nd
BANK HOLIDAY IN SCOTLAND. FULL MOON

I felt rotten today. It's my mother's fault for singing "My Way" at two o'clock in the morning at the top of the stairs. Just my luck to have a mother like her. There is a chance my parents could be alcoholics. Next year I could be in a children's home.

The dog got its own back on my father. It jumped up and knocked down his model ship, then ran into the garden with the rigging tangled in its feet. My father kept saying, "Three months' work down the drain," over and over again.

The spot on my chin is getting bigger. It's my mother's fault for not knowing about vitamins.

Saturday January 3rd

I shall go mad through lack of sleep! My father has banned the dog from the house so it barked outside my window all night. Just my luck! My father shouted a swear-word at it. If he's not careful he will get done by the police for obscene language.

I think the spot is a boil. Just my luck to have it where everybody can see it. I pointed out to my mother that I hadn't had any vitamin C today. She said, "Go and buy an orange, then." This is typical.

She still hasn't worn the lurex apron.

I will be glad to get back to school.

Sunday January 4th
SECOND AFTER CHRISTMAS

My father has got the flu. I'm not surprised with the diet

we get. My mother went out in the rain to get him a vitamin C drink, but as I told her, "It's too late now." It's a miracle we don't get scurvy. My mother says she can't see anything on my chin, but this is guilt because of the diet.

The dog has run off because my mother didn't close the gate. I have broken the arm on the stereo. Nobody knows yet, and with a bit of luck my father will be ill for a long time. He is the only one who uses it apart from me. No sign of the apron.

Monday January 5th

The dog hasn't come back yet. It is peaceful without it. My mother rang the police and gave a description of the dog. She made it sound worse than it actually is: straggly hair over its eyes and all that. I really think the police have got better things to do than look for dogs, such as catching murderers. I told my mother this but she still rang them. Serve her right if she was murdered because of the dog.

My father is still lazing about in bed. He is supposed to be ill, but I noticed he is still smoking!

Nigel came round today. He has got a tan from his Christmas holiday. I think Nigel will be ill soon from the shock of the cold in England. I think Nigel's parents were wrong to take him abroad.

He hasn't got a single spot yet.

Tuesday January 6th
EPIPHANY. NEW MOON

The dog is in trouble!

It knocked a meter-reader off his bike and messed all the cards up. So now we will all end up in court I expect. A policeman said we must keep the dog under control and asked how long it had been lame. My mother said it wasn't lame, and examined it. There was a tiny model pirate trapped in its left front paw.

The dog was pleased when my mother took the pirate out and it jumped up the policeman's tunic with its muddy paws. My mother fetched a cloth from the kitchen but it had strawberry jam on it where I had wiped the knife, so the tunic was worse than ever. The policeman went then. I'm sure he swore. I could report him for that.

I will look up *Epiphany* in my new dictionary.

Wednesday January 7th

Nigel came round on his new bike this morning. It has got a water bottle, a milometer, a speedometer, a yellow saddle, and very thin racing wheels. It's wasted on Nigel. He only goes to the shops and back on it. If I had it, I would go all over the country and have an experience.

My spot or boil has reached its peak. Surely it can't get any bigger! I found a word in my dictionary that describes my father. It is *malingerer*. He is still in bed guzzling vitamin C.

The dog is locked in the coal shed.

Epiphany is something to do with the three wise men. Big deal!

Thursday January 8th

Now my mother has got the flu. This means that I have to look after them both. Just my luck!

I have been up and down the stairs all day. I cooked a big dinner for them tonight: two poached eggs with beans, and tinned semolina pudding. (It's a good job I wore the green lurex apron because the poached eggs escaped out of the pan and got all over me.) I nearly said something when I saw they hadn't eaten *any* of it. They can't be that ill. I gave it to the dog in the coal shed. My grandmother is coming tomorrow morning, so I had to clean the burnt saucepans, then take the dog for a walk. It was half-past eleven before I got to bed. No wonder I am short for my age.

I have decided against medicine for a career.

Friday January 9th

It was cough, cough, cough last night. If it wasn't one it was the other. You'd think they'd show some considera-tion after the hard day I'd had.

My grandma came and was disgusted with the state of the house. I showed her my room which is always neat and tidy and she gave me fifty pence. I showed her all the empty drink bottles in the dustbin and she was disgusted.

My grandma let the dog out of the coal shed. She said my mother was cruel to lock it up. The dog was sick on the kitchen floor. My grandma locked it up again.

She squeezed the spot on my chin. It has made it worse. I told grandma about the green apron and grandma said that she bought my mother a one hundred per cent acrylic cardigan every Christmas and my mother had *never ever* worn one of them!

Saturday January 10th

A.M. Now the dog is ill! It keeps being sick so the vet has got to come. My father told me not to tell the vet that the dog had been locked in the coal shed for two days.

I have put a plaster over the spot to stop germs getting in it from the dog.

The vet has taken the dog away. He says he thinks it has got an obstruction and will need an emergency operation.

My grandma has had a row with my mother and gone home. My grandma found the Christmas cardigans all cut up in the duster bag. It is disgusting when people are starving.

Mr Lucas from next door has been in to see my mother and father who are still in bed. He brought a "get well" card and some flowers for my mother. My mother sat up in bed in a nightie that showed a lot of her chest. She talked to Mr Lucas in a yukky voice. My father pretended to be asleep.

Nigel brought his records round. He is into punk, but I don't see the point if you can't hear the words. Anyway I think I'm turning into an intellectual. It must be all the worry.

P.M. I went to see how the dog is. It has had its operation. The vet showed me a plastic bag with lots of yukky things in it. There was a lump of coal, the fir tree from the Christmas cake, and the model pirates from my father's ship. One of the pirates was waving a cutlass which must have been very painful for the dog. The dog looks a lot better. It can come home in two days, worse luck.

My father was having a row with my grandma on the phone about the empty bottles in the dustbin when I got home.

Mr Lucas was upstairs talking to my mother. When Mr Lucas went, my father went upstairs and had an argument with my mother and made her cry. My father is in a bad mood. This means he is feeling better. I made my mother a cup of tea without her asking. This made her cry as well. You can't please some people!

The spot is still there.

Sunday January 11th
FIRST AFTER EPIPHANY

Now I *know* I am an intellectual. I saw Malcolm Muggeridge on the television last night, and I understood nearly every word. It all adds up. A bad home, poor diet, not liking punk. I think I will join the library and see what happens.

It is a pity there aren't any more intellectuals living round here. Mr Lucas wears corduroy trousers, but he's an insurance man. Just my luck.

The first what after Epiphany?

Monday January 12th

The dog is back. It keeps licking its stitches, so when I am eating I sit with my back to it.

My mother got up this morning to make the dog a bed to sleep in until it's better. It is made out of a cardboard box that used to contain packets of soap powder. My father said this would make the dog sneeze and burst its stitches, and the vet would charge even more to stitch it back up again. They had a row about the box, then my father went on about Mr Lucas. Though what Mr Lucas has to do with the dog's bed is a mystery to me.

Tuesday January 13th

My father has gone back to work. Thank God! I don't know how my mother sticks him.

Mr Lucas came in this morning to see if my mother needed any help in the house. He is very kind. Mrs Lucas was next door cleaning the outside windows. The ladder didn't look very safe. I have written to Malcolm Muggeridge, c/o the BBC, asking him what to do about being an intellectual. I hope he writes back soon because I'm getting fed up being one on my own. I have written a poem, and it only took me two minutes. Even the famous poets take longer than that. It is called "The Tap", but it isn't really about a tap, it's very deep, and about life and stuff like that.

The Tap, by Adrian Mole
The tap drips and keeps me awake,
In the morning there will be a lake.
For the want of a washer the carpet will spoil,
Then for another my father will toil.
My father could snuff it while he is at work.
Dad, fit a washer don't be a burk!

I showed it to my mother, but she laughed. She isn't very bright. She still hasn't washed my PE shorts, and it is school tomorrow. She is not like the mothers on television.

Wednesday January 14th

Joined the library. Got *Care of the Skin*, *Origin of Species*, and a book by a woman my mother is always going on about. It is called *Pride and Prejudice*, by a woman called Jane Austen. I could tell the librarian was impressed. Perhaps she is an intellectual like me. She didn't look at my spot, so perhaps it is getting smaller. About time!

Mr Lucas was in the kitchen drinking coffee with my mother. The room was full of smoke. They were laughing, but when I went in, they stopped.

Mrs Lucas was next door cleaning the drains. She looked as if she was in a bad mood. I think Mr and Mrs Lucas have got an unhappy marriage. Poor Mr Lucas!

None of the teachers at school have noticed that I am intellectual. They will be sorry when I am famous. There is a new girl in our class. She sits next to me in Geography. She is all right. Her name is Pandora, but she likes being called "Box". Don't ask me why. I might fall in love with her. It's time I fell in love, after all I am 13¾ years old.

LITTLE BY LITTLE

JEAN LITTLE

I LOOKED UP from my grade five reader and smiled. I liked Miss Marr a lot. And, even though we had only met an hour ago, I thought she liked me, too.

She was young and pretty and she had a gentle voice. But that was not all. Like Mr Johnston, she had had polio. As I listened to her passing out books behind me, I could hear her limping, first a quick step, then a slow one. The sound made me feel a little less lonely. My teacher would understand how it felt to be the only cross-eyed girl in Victory School.

"This is your desk, Jean," she had said.

It sat, all by itself, right up against the front black-board. I was supposed to be able to see better there. I had not yet managed to make anyone understand that if I wanted to read what was written on the board, I would have to stand up so that my face was only inches away from the writing. Then I would have to walk back and forth, following the words not only with my eyes but with my entire body. If the writing were up at the top of the board, I would have to stand on tiptoe or even climb on a chair to be able to decipher it. If it were near the bottom, I would have to crouch down.

I remembered Miss Bogart printing large, thick, yellow letters on a green chalkboard. That had been so different. These dusty grey boards looked almost the same colour as the thin, white scratches Miss Marr's chalk made. Her small, neat words were composed of letters that flowed into each other, too, which made reading them even harder.

I would not explain. How could I? She might make me climb and crouch to read the words.

I stood out far too much as it was. All the desks except mine were nailed to the floor in five straight rows. The seats flipped up when you slid out of them. They were attached to the desk behind. On top was a trough for your pencil and, in the right-hand corner, an inkwell which Miss Marr kept filled from a big ink bottle with a long spout. All the desk lids were a dark wine colour.

My desk was new and varnished a shiny golden brown. It had been provided for me because, in theory, it could be moved to wherever I could see best. It was, however, far too heavy and unwieldy for Miss Marr or me to shift. All that special desk did was single me out even more.

I turned sideways in my new desk so that I could watch Miss Marr and caught sight of Shirley Russell instead. If only she would notice me!

Shirley had about her the magic of a story. She and her brother Ian had come from England to stay with their aunt and uncle and be safe from the bombing. She had joined our class near the end of grade four. Shirley had a lovely voice, with an accent like the child movie actress Margaret O'Brien's. She also had golden ringlets, longer and fairer than Shirley Temple's. She was a War Guest. She was different, too, but everybody wanted to be her friend.

"Face front, Jean," Miss Marr said. "Here are your spelling words."

She had typed them for me on a big print typewriter. I

bent over them, drawing each letter on the roof of my mouth with the tip of my tongue. I had discovered that this helped me to remember them. It also helped fill in time.

When the bell rang for recess, Miss Marr astonished me by saying to Shirley Russell, "This is Jean Little, Shirley. She can't see well. Would you be her friend and help her to get into the right line when it's time to come back inside?"

Shirley smiled sweetly and nodded her golden head. I could not believe this was really happening. Shirley Russell was actually going to be my friend. At last I was going to have a girl to do things with, and not just any girl. The War Guest herself!

We marched down the stairs and went out into the girls' side of the playground. I turned to Shirley, my smile shy, my heart singing.

Shirley scowled. Just under her breath, so that nobody but me could hear, she snarled, "You keep away from me. Get lost!"

Then she turned and ran.

"Be my partner, Shirley, and I'll give you my Crackerjack prize," I heard one girl call out.

There was a hubbub of offered bribes and vows of eternal friendship. Nobody looked in my direction.

I stood where I was, stunned into immobility. I should have guessed, perhaps, that our teacher had asked the impossible of the English girl. She was popular at the moment, but if she had me trailing after her, her accent might suddenly cease to be interesting and just be weird. She was a foreigner, after all, and she knew it.

Before any of them had time to notice me watching them, I walked away to the far side of the playground. I leaned up against a tall tree and stared off into the distance, as though I had my mind on things other than silly grade five girls. To keep myself from crying, I began talking to the tree that was supporting me.

"Are you lonely, too, tree?" I murmured. "If you are, I'll come every day and talk to you. We could be friends."

As I drew a shaking breath, much like a sob, I heard a gentle rustle above my head. I glanced up. The leafy branches seemed to nod to me.

You can count on a tree, I told myself. A tree is better than a person.

But I knew it was not true.

When we were supposed to line up to march in again, I heard Shirley's laugh and tagged on the end of the right line. I counted my steps on the way in. I'd find it tomorrow without any help from Shirley Russell.

Back at my desk, I heard Miss Marr ask two people to pass out pieces of paper. Staring down at the blank sheet, I hoped we were going to draw or write a composition.

"We're going to have a mental arithmetic test," Miss Marr said. "Write down the numbers 1 to 10 on your paper."

I bent my arm around my sheet, shielding it from prying eyes, even though the others were not close to me. I had a sinking feeling the test she was talking about would involve those horrible times tables everybody but me had mastered in grade three. I picked up the special fat pencil Miss Marr had given me and did as I had been told. As I waited for the first question, I clutched the pencil so tightly that my knuckles whitened.

"Question one," said Miss Marr. "8 x 3."

I began to add. Eight and eight were . . . sixteen? Or was it fourteen?

Three and three are six, I muttered inside my head, changing my method of attack. I turned down two fingers so that I would know when I reached eight.

"Question two," Miss Marr said. "6 x 4."

I gave up on question one and began to add fours. I had reached twelve and four are sixteen when she went on to question three.

When she reached question ten, I stared down at my paper in dismay. All that was written on it were the numbers 1 to 10 in a neat column. I had not managed to

get even one answer.

"Since this is the first day, you can each mark your own paper," she said. "What is it, Ruth?"

"Can I sharpen my pencil?" Ruth Dayton's voice asked.

"Yes. But hurry up. You are keeping us all waiting."

As she passed behind me, Ruth glanced over my shoulder. I did not notice her small hiss of astonishment as she took in the fact that I had not answered a single question.

"The answer to question one is twenty-four," the teacher said as Ruth regained her seat.

I knew that behind my back, forty pencils were checking the answer. I had to do something to look busy. With painstaking neatness, I pencilled in 24 beside the number 1.

"If you have 24 beside the number 1," said my new teacher, "check it right."

I stared down at my page. There, right next to the 1 was written 24. Feeling a little like a sleepwalker, unable to stop herself, I put a check mark next to the answer my teacher had just dictated. After all, she had *not* said, "If you got the answer right . . . " She had said, "If you have the number 24 beside the number 1 . . . " And I did.

"The correct answer for Number 2 is also 24," she said then. I wrote that down.

"If you have the answer 24 beside the number 2, check it right."

We worked our way down the sheet. First she would tell us the answer. I would write it down. Then she would instruct us to "check it right", and I would put a neat check mark on the paper.

When the others had finished marking their answers right or wrong, Miss Marr said, "Raise your hand if you have ten answers checked right."

I looked at my arithmetic paper. There they were, all ten answers checked right. I raised my hand. As I did so, I expected something dramatic to happen, a thunderbolt to strike me dead or a huge voice to roar, "*Jean Little, what have you done?*" Nothing of the kind disturbed Miss Marr's classroom. The teacher looked around at the eight or nine raised hands.

"Good for you," she said.

I snatched my hand down and stared hard at a broken piece of chalk lying in the chalk trough. I did not check to see whether anybody admitted to having none checked right. I was sure I was the only one who would have missed them all.

As she began a geography lesson, I felt relief wash over me. Mental arithmetic was at an end, for that day, at least. Perhaps everything was going to be all right.

My happiness lasted until noon.

Ruth and Stella came marching up to my desk while I was putting away my books. They stared at me with contempt.

"I saw you," Ruth said.

"What a cheat!" Stella put in. Her eyes were gleaming.

"Saw me what?" I said feebly. "I don't know what you're talking about. I didn't cheat."

"You might as well save your breath," Stella sneered. "Ruth *saw* you and so did I. You copied down the answers after she said them out loud."

"Are you going to tell on me?" I heard, and despised,

the bleat of panic in my voice. They had me at their mercy and we all knew it.

"Do you think we would tattle?" Stella said, as though such a thing had never been known to happen. "We won't tell."

I cheered up too soon. She had not finished.

"But if you don't tell her yourself what a cheater you are, nobody in this class will ever speak to you again. We don't intend to be friends with a cheater."

I had no choice. I longed for friends. In spite of Shirley's snub, I still hoped that someday it might happen. I couldn't risk turning the entire class against me.

Miss Marr was at her desk. I walked up to stand beside it, moving slowly, trying hard to think of a way to confess that would satisfy my class and not make Miss Marr hate me.

Ruth and Stella lurked near enough to hear what I said. I stood by my teacher's elbow until she looked up. Then I took a deep breath and began. I stammered and stuttered, but at last she took in what I was mumbling. She told me to sit down. Then she waved Stella and Ruth away.

"You two are supposed to be on your way home," she said, her voice a little sharp. "Run along."

They went as slowly as they dared, but until they were well out of earshot, Miss Marr ignored me. She sharpened a pencil, then two. Finally she turned and looked at me.

"I saw what you did, Jean," she said.

I gasped. Had she watched me cheat and said nothing? I could not believe it.

She sat down near me and went on quietly.

"I don't think you meant to cheat, did you? It just happened . . . when you could not get the answers fast enough to keep up. Wasn't that the way it was?"

"Yes. That's just what happened," I told her, staring at the floor and trying not to cry. "I'm no good at my times tables . . ."

"You won't ever do it again, will you?"

I shook my head violently.

"Never ever!"

"Then we'll just forget it this time," she told me. "And you'd better get busy learning your tables."

"I will," I promised. "Oh, I will."

I positively ran from the room. But when I got outside, I found Ruth and Stella and four or five others waiting.

"What did she say?" they demanded.

I opened my mouth to tell them how nice Miss Marr had been. Then I stopped to think. The minute the other kids found out that I had not got the strap or been sent to the principal, they would all decide she was a "soft" teacher, easy to put one over on.

"I won't tell you," I said as bravely as I could, "but she was mad!"

Ruth seemed impressed. Stella gave me a scornful glance. But as she reached out to grab by hand and turn it palm up to see if it had strap marks on it, Jamie came around the corner of the school. He glanced in our direction, was about to go on, and then turned back.

"What's going on?" he demanded.

"He's my brother," I told them, feeling as though Robin Hood himself had come to my rescue.

The girls backed away.

"We're not hurting her," Ruth declared, but she was moving off step by step.

The rest melted away without a word. Jamie gave me an annoyed, big-brotherly look.

"You'd better hurry up or you'll be late for dinner," he said. "You can't walk with me."

I smiled. "I know," I told him humbly.

I knew better than to expect an eighth grade boy to walk with a mere fifth grade girl. Yet just knowing he was in the world, I felt protected all the way home.

SAM'S STORM

BETSY BYARS

"I AM IN PAIN!" Sam yelled at the top of his lungs.

There was no answer.

"I am in great pain!"

Again, no answer. The only sound in the big empty house was Sam's sigh.

He looked down at his red, swollen feet, propped on separate pillows. He realized that he now knew the exact meaning of the word "throb". His feet throbbed. He had five hornet stings on one and four on the other. And they throbbed.

"I am in pain and agony!" he yelled, even though there was no one to hear him. The entire family had gone in the pickup truck to see a 75-pound snapping turtle Mr Johnson had pulled out of his fishing pond.

He had watched them drive away, his cousins in the back of the truck, laughing and excited, his grandparents in the front.

"You're sure you don't mind being left alone?" his grandmother had asked.

"I don't mind," he had answered, in a way that should have let her know he minded a lot.

"We'll be back in less than an hour."

"Don't worry about me."

"Here's some lemonade and cookies if you get hungry. Here are two aspirin in case your feet hurt."

In case they hurt! he had wanted to yell. What do you think they've been doing all day? I am in agony!

"This is the Johnsons' phone number, where we'll be, and the phone's right here at your elbow. We'll be back before the thunderstorms."

Every afternoon since he'd been at his grandparents' farm, they had had thunderstorms – big, powerful storms with booming thunder and streaks of lightning. The only one who hated the storms more than Sam was his grandparents' big black dog, Bull.

"Now, you're sure you—"

"I'll be fine!"

Actually, it was amazing how little sympathy he was getting. His feet were as big as balloons. His toes were like sausages. Each hornet sting was a white welt in the red, swollen flesh.

And yet, because it was his own fault, because he had gone out in the yard barefoot, nobody seemed to care. How was he to know hornets made nests in the ground? How was he to know he could be stung, and that, while he was hopping in fear and pain from one foot to the other, he could be stung eight more times?

His cousins had known, but they were farm kids. He was from the city. He thought hornets only made nests in trees. His eyes filled with tears of sympathy for himself.

He heard scratching at the screen door. "Bull?" he called. "Is that you?"

The only time Bull ever wanted to come into the house was when a storm was coming. Bull, his grandfather said, was better than the weatherman at predicting storms.

"When that dog wants in the house, you can bet a

storm's coming. And the more he wants in, the worse the storm's going to be. Just before the '84 tornado, he came *through* the screen door."

"Why is he so afraid of storms?" Sam had asked.

"He blew in here one night during a storm. That's the way we got him. We went out one morning, and the yard was covered with limbs and wood, buckets and stray chickens, every kind of thing. And under the front steps was Bull. Since that day, he hasn't been able to abide a storm."

"Didn't you try to find out who he belonged to?"

"We asked around. But if a dog gets blown away in a storm like that, he can't ever find his way home. He gets disoriented. He could live a half-mile away, and he still wouldn't be able to find it."

Bull barked at the front door.

"I'd let you in," Sam called, "but I'm in agony!"

Sam glanced out the window. To the east the sky was bright blue, the clouds white.

"Anyway, there's no storm in sight, Bull," he called.

Bull was not comforted. He barked again and scratched at the screen. Sam rested his head against the back of the chair. He looked at the phone. Now would be a good time to call his parents and tell them about his feet. He had the number of their hotel in San Francisco. Maybe he could pretend to be calling to see if they were having fun, and then just mention casually that he had stepped on nine hornets and . . .

Bull's face appeared in the window. For a huge, strong dog – that was how he got the name Bull – he could look terrified. His tongue was lolling out of his mouth, drops of saliva were dropping onto the sill, his eyes bulged, his whole body trembled.

At that moment a long, low rumble of thunder came from the west. Bull threw back his head and howled.

Suddenly Sam was uneasy, too. Maybe, he thought, I am sitting here looking at this patch of blue sky, thinking there is no danger, while behind me . . .

He glanced quickly over his shoulder. Through the hall, he could see the edge of the dining-room window. The sky there was black.

He turned and met Bull's pleading eyes. "Stop looking at me like that. I can't do anything."

Bull barked twice, the last bark ending in a howl.

"I'm telling you, I'm helpless." He broke off to listen to the newest roll of thunder. The sound was moving closer. This storm was coming faster than usual.

"Now you're making me nervous," he told Bull.

The dog put his huge paws against the screen and began to dig. Slits opened in the screen. There was another roll of thunder. Bull dug faster.

"Stop it!" Sam yelled. But Bull was beyond hearing a command.

The slits in the screen were lengthening. Soon the screen

was in ribbons. Bull began to pry his way through. He jumped in, hit the floor, and without pausing ran for the chair where Sam sat.

"No!" Sam yelled, holding out his arms to protect himself. He recalled that Bull had jumped onto his grandfather's lap the afternoon before. "Look at my big baby," his grandfather had said.

"No!"

In one leap, Bull cleared the footstool and was on Sam's lap. The pain jarred Sam's feet. Tears came to his eyes. "Get down!" he moaned, but Bull was curled into a ball of fear. His soft, pleading eyes looked up at Sam.

With a sigh, Sam gave in. Getting Bull off his lap would be more painful than letting him stay. "All right, but be still."

Actually, it was comforting to have the big dog on his lap. He rested his arms on Bull's trembling shoulders. "I know how you feel, pal, because I don't care for storms either."

There was another crash of thunder. This time the sound echoed from cloud to cloud, as if it were building force. Bull tried to bury his head under Sam's arm.

At that moment, wind swept through the house, blowing through the open windows. Upstairs, a door slammed. On the porch, the hanging baskets of plants began hitting the rail. The curtains were drawn tight against the screens.

Sam picked up the phone. He was going to call the Johnsons. He looked for the number, but it had blown across the room in the first rush of wind.

"Why don't they come home?" he asked. "Don't they see the storm? How long does it take to look at a turtle?"

The wind at his neck had stiffened. Outside, branches blew against the house. A chair on the porch turned over with a bang. The porch swing crashed against the house.

"We ought to go to the basement," he said. Every afternoon his grandmother listened to the storm, judged it, and said, "Well, it's not bad enough for us to go to the basement."

"This one," he told Bull, "is bad enough for us to go to the basement."

Turning sideways, he dumped Bull on the floor. Bull waited in a crouch, tail between his huge legs, ears flat. Then he crawled under the nearest table.

Sam slipped off the chair and landed hard on his knees. He too waited, crouched in pain. Slowly, he straightened.

"Come on," he told Bull. The dog only trembled harder.

Sam crossed the room, grimacing with pain, and grabbed Bull's thick collar. "Come on."

Bull pulled back, bracing himself, not wanting to leave the safety of the table. "Come on!" The floor was slick and well waxed, and Bull slid out. Sam dragged him into the hall.

Through the front door, Sam saw the blackest sky he had ever seen in his life. Drops of water the size of marbles began to pelt the porch. The old oak tree groaned in the wind.

Sam struggled down the hall, dragging Bull with him over the slick floor. Outside, an oak limb crashed against the house. Glass shattered.

At last Sam's hand closed around the knob to the basement door. He pulled, and in a rush Bull slipped past him, down the steps, and behind the water heater. "Thanks for waiting," Sam said.

He crawled down two steps, and the wind slammed the door behind him. He was in darkness now. He felt his way down the stairs, step by step, like a small child. As he got to the bottom, he heard a noise overhead, a crash so loud it seemed the whole world had been split apart. He covered his head with his hands and waited for the worst.

"Sam!"

He lifted his head.

"Sam?"

"I'm in the basement." He had no idea how long he had been here, waiting out the storm – maybe an hour.

The basement door opened, and Sam looked up at his grandfather. "Are you all right, Sam?"

"Yes."

Behind his grandfather there was no hall, mirror, or rose wallpaper. Behind his grandfather was a solid wall of leaves. "What happened?"

"The oak tree," his grandfather said, choking on the words, unable to continue.

Sam began to climb the stairs on his knees. On the top step, he stopped. There was no way to get through the hall.

"The living room," his grandfather said, pointing helplessly. "I thought you—" Again he had to stop.

Sam was stunned. He said, "The tree fell on the living room? What's grandma going to say. She loved that tree. She loved this house."

His grandfather shook his head.

"It can be fixed, can't it?"

"Maybe."

Sam heard a noise on the stairs, and he looked down. Bull was coming up. As the big dog squeezed past, Sam scratched him behind the ears. Bull disappeared into the branches.

"We'd better let your grandma know you're safe," his grandfather said. "You're what she's worried about."

"I'm fine." When he said it this time, it was true.

"Will you be all right till I get back? I have to walk. Trees are down all over the road."

Sam nodded. His grandfather went to the kitchen door and stood for a moment, hunched over like an old man, looking at the ruins. Keeping to the wall, Sam took slow, painful steps on his swollen feet. He paused beside his grandfather at the kitchen door.

From here he could see the damage. The huge oak tree had split the side of the house and crushed the room where he had sat nursing his swollen feet.

He held onto the door to steady himself. He felt disoriented. Like Bull, he could never get back to the place where he had sat an hour before, yelling, "I am in pain."

Bull was running around the tree, sniffing the broken branches, leaping over the leaves, wild with excitement. The huge ball of roots and dirt was as high as the porch roof.

"One thing," his grandfather said. "You probably saved old Bull's life."

Sam hesitated and then said, truthfully, "We saved each other."

His grandfather nodded, squared his shoulders, and went down the steps.

ANNE'S HISTORY

L. M. MONTGOMERY

from Anne of Green Gables

Matthew and Marilla Cuthbert of Avonlea need help on their farm, so they offer to take a boy from the orphan asylum. Their friend, Mrs Spencer of White Sands, is to pick out a likely boy for them. But a mistake is made and they are sent instead a talkative eleven-year-old girl, Anne Shirley. Marilla is horrified and the next day she drives Anne over to Mrs Spencer to find out how the misunderstanding occurred.

"DO YOU KNOW," said Anne confidentially, "I've made up my mind to enjoy this drive. It's been my experience that you can nearly always enjoy things if you make up your mind firmly that you will. Of course, you must make it up *firmly*. I am not going to think about going back to the asylum while we're having our drive. I'm just going to think about the drive. Oh, look, there's one little early wild rose out! Isn't it lovely? Don't you think it must be glad to be a rose? Wouldn't it be nice if roses could talk? I'm sure they could tell us such lovely things. And isn't pink the most bewitching colour in the world? I love it, but I can't wear it. Redheaded people can't wear pink, not even in imagination. Did you ever know of anybody whose hair was red when she was young, but got to be another colour when she grew up?"

"No, I don't know as I ever did," said Marilla mercilessly, "and I shouldn't think it likely to happen in your case, either."

Anne sighed.

"Well, that is another hope gone. My life is a perfect graveyard of buried hopes. That's a sentence I read in a book once, and I say it over to comfort myself whenever I'm disappointed in anything."

"I don't see where the comforting comes in myself," said Marilla.

"Why, because it sounds so nice and romantic, just as if I were a heroine in a book, you know. I am so fond of romantic things, and a graveyard full of buried hopes is about as romantic a thing as one can imagine, isn't it? I'm rather glad I have one. Are we going across the Lake of Shining Waters today?"

"We're not going over Barry's pond, if that's what you mean by your Lake of Shining Waters. We're going by the shore road."

"Shore road sounds nice," said Anne dreamily. "Is it as nice as it sounds? Just when you said 'shore road' I saw it in a picture in my mind, as quick as that! And White Sands is a pretty name, too; but I don't like it as well as Avonlea. Avonlea is a lovely name. It just sounds like music. How far is it to White Sands?"

"It's five miles; and as you're evidently bent on talking you might as well talk to some purpose by telling me what you know about yourself."

"Oh, what I *know* about myself isn't really worth telling," said Anne eagerly. "If you'll only let me tell you what I *imagine* about myself you'll think it ever so much more interesting."

"No, I don't want any of your imaginings. Just you stick

79

to bald facts. Begin at the beginning. Where were you born and how old are you?"

"I was eleven last March," said Anne, resigning herself to bald facts with a little sigh. "And I was born in Bolingbroke, Nova Scotia. My father's name was Walter Shirley, and he was a teacher in the Bolingbroke High School. My mother's name was Bertha Shirley. Aren't Walter and Bertha lovely names? I'm so glad my parents had nice names. It would be a real disgrace to have a father named – well, say Jedediah, wouldn't it?"

"I guess it doesn't matter what a person's name is as long as he behaves himself," said Marilla, feeling herself called upon to inculcate a good and useful moral.

"Well, I don't know." Anne looked thoughtful. "I read in a book once that a rose by any other name would smell as sweet, but I've never been able to believe it. I don't believe a rose *would* be as nice if it was called a thistle or a skunk-cabbage. I suppose my father could have been a good man even if he had been called Jedediah; but I'm sure it would have been a cross. Well, my mother was a teacher in the High School, too, but when she married father she gave up teaching, of course. A husband was enough responsibility. Mrs Thomas said that they were a pair of babies and as poor as church mice. They went to live in a weeny-teeny little yellow house in Bolingbroke. I've never seen that house, but I've imagined it thousands of times. I think it must have had honeysuckle over the parlour window and lilacs in the front yard and lilies of the valley just inside the gate. Yes, and muslin curtains in all the windows. Muslin curtains give a house such an air. I was born in that house. Mrs Thomas said I was the homeliest baby she ever saw, I was so scrawny and tiny and nothing but eyes, but that Mother thought I was perfectly beautiful. I should think a mother would be a better judge than a poor woman who came in to scrub, wouldn't you? I'm glad she was satisfied with me anyhow; I would feel so sad if I thought I was a disappointment to her – because she didn't

live very long after that, you see. She died of fever when I
was just three months old, I do wish she'd lived long
enough for me to remember calling her mother. I think it
would be so sweet to say 'Mother', don't you? And Father
died four days afterwards from fever, too. That left me an
orphan and folks were at their wits' end, so Mrs Thomas
said, what to do with me. You see, nobody wanted me
even then. It seems to be my fate. Father and Mother had
both come from places far away and it was well known
they hadn't any relatives living. Finally Mrs Thomas said
she'd take me, though she was poor and had a drunken
husband. She brought me up by hand. Do you know if
there is anything in being brought up by hand that ought
to make people who are brought up that way better than
other people? Because whenever I was naughty Mrs
Thomas would ask me how I could be such a bad girl when
she had brought me up by hand – reproachful-like.

"Mr and Mrs Thomas moved away from Bolingbroke to
Marysville, and I lived with them until I was eight years
old. I helped look after the Thomas children – there were
four of them younger than me – and I can tell you they
took a lot of looking after. Then Mr Thomas was killed
falling under a train, and his mother offered to take Mrs
Thomas and the children, but she didn't want me. Mrs
Thomas was at *her* wits' end, so she said, what to do with
me. Then Mrs Hammond from up the river came down
and said she'd take me, seeing I was handy with children,
and I went up the river to live with her in a little clearing
among the stumps. It was a very lonesome place. I'm sure I
could never have lived there if I hadn't an imagination. Mr
Hammond worked a little saw-mill up there, and Mrs
Hammond had eight children. She had twins three times. I
like babies in moderation, but twins three times in
succession is *too much*. I told Mrs Hammond so firmly,
when the last pair came. I used to get so dreadfully tired
carrying them about.

"I lived up river with Mrs Hammond over two years,

and them Mr Hammond died and Mrs Hammond broke up house-keeping. She divided her children among her relatives and went to the States. I had to go to the asylum in Hopeton, because nobody would take me. They didn't want me at the asylum, either; they said they were overcrowded as it was. But they had to take me and I was there four months until Mrs Spencer came."

Anne finished up with another sigh, of relief this time. Evidently she did not like talking about her experiences in a world that had not wanted her.

"Did you ever go to school?" demanded Marilla, turning the sorrel mare down the shore road.

"Not a great deal. I went a little the last year I stayed with Mrs Thomas. When I went up river we were so far from a school that I couldn't walk it in winter and there was vacation in summer, so I could only go in the spring and fall. But of course, I went while I was at the asylum. I can read pretty well and I know ever so many pieces of poetry off by heart – 'The Battle of Hohenlinden' and 'Edinburgh after Flodden,' and 'Bingen on the Rhine,' and lots of the *Lady of the Lake* and most of *The Seasons*, by James Thompson. Don't you just love poetry that gives you a crinkly feeling up and down your back? There is a piece in the Fifth Reader – 'The Downfall of Poland' – that is just full of thrills. Of course, I wasn't in the Fifth Reader – I was only in the Fourth – but the big girls used to lend me theirs to read."

"Were those women – Mrs Thomas and Mrs Hammond – good to you?" asked Marilla, looking at Anne out of the corner of her eye.

"O-o-o-h," faltered Anne. Her sensitive little face suddenly flushed scarlet and embarrassment sat on her brow. "Oh, they *meant* to be – I know they meant to be just as good and kind as possible. And when people mean to be good to you, you don't mind very much when they're not quite – always. They had a good deal to worry them, you know. It's very trying to have a drunken husband, you see; and it must be very trying to have twins three times in succession, don't you think? But I feel sure they meant to be good to me."

Marilla asked no more questions. Anne gave herself up to a silent rapture over the shore road and Marilla guided the sorrel abstractedly while she pondered deeply. Pity was suddenly stirring in her heart for the child. What a starved, unloved life she had had – a life of drudgery and poverty and neglect; for Marilla was shrewd enough to read between the lines of Anne's history and divine the truth. No wonder she had been so delighted at the prospect of a real home. It was a pity she had to be sent back. What if she, Marilla, should indulge Matthew's unaccountable whim and let her stay? He was set on it; and the child seemed a nice, teachable little thing.

"She's got too much to say," thought Marilla, "but she

might be trained out of that. And there's nothing rude or slangy in what she does say. She's ladylike. It's likely her people were nice folks."

The shore road was "woodsy and wild and lonesome." On the right hand, scrub firs, their spirits quite unbroken by long years of tussle with the gulf winds, grew thickly. On the left were the steep red sandstone cliffs, so near the track in places that a mare of less steadiness than sorrel might have tried the nerves of the people behind her. Down at the base of the cliffs were heaps of surf-worn rocks or little sandy coves inlaid with pebbles as with ocean jewels; beyond lay the sea, shimmering and blue, and over it soared the gulls, their pinions flashing silvery in the sunlight.

"Isn't the sea wonderful?" said Anne, rousing from a long, wide-eyed silence. "Once, when I lived in Marysville, Mr Thomas hired an express-wagon and took us all to spend the day at the shore ten miles away. I enjoyed every moment of that day, even if I had to look after the children all the time. I lived it over in happy dreams for years. But this shore is nicer than the Marysville shore. Aren't those gulls splendid? Would you like to be a gull? I think I would – that is if I couldn't be a human girl. Don't you think it would be nice to wake up at sunrise and swoop down over the water and away out over that lovely blue all day; and then at night to fly back to one's nest? Oh, I can just imagine myself doing it. What big house is that just ahead, please?"

"That's the White Sands Hotel. Mr Kirke runs it, but the season hasn't begun yet. There are heaps of Americans come there for the summer. They think this shore is just about right."

"I was afraid it might be Mrs Spencer's place," said Anne mournfully. "I don't want to get there. Somehow, it will seem like the end of everything."

MAY I HAVE YOUR AUTOGRAPH?

MARJORIE SHARMAT

I AM SITTING in an overstuffed chair in the lobby of The Dominion Imperial International Hotel. So help me, that's really the name. I am surrounded by overgrown ferns, ugly but expensive floral carpeting, chandeliers that make me think of *The Phantom of the Opera*, stuck-up hotel employees in silly-looking uniforms who give me dirty looks – and nobody my age. Except my friend Wendy, who dragged me here.

Wendy is here to meet a guy, but he doesn't know it. In fact, he's never heard of Wendy. But that doesn't stop her from being in love with him. Well, maybe not in love. I think love is for people you've at least met. Wendy has never met Craig the Cat. That's the name of the guy. At least that's his stage name. He's a rock star who's been famous for over six months. Even *my* parents have heard of him.

Wendy is here to get Craig the Cat's autograph on his latest album. On the album jacket, Craig is wearing a black cat costume and he's sitting on a garbage pail with a bottle of spilled milk beside him. He is holding his guitar in his long, furry arms.

Wendy constantly talks about Craig the Cat. But it was like discussing something that was going on in another time frame, on another continent. I didn't mind. It was nicely, safely unreal. Until Craig the Cat came to town today. He's giving a string of benefit performances across the country for some kind of animal group that's devoted to saving "the cats."

"That includes everything from alley cats to exotic tigers," Wendy told me.

"How do you know?"

"I know."

We used our allowance money to buy tickets. That landed us exactly five rows from the back of the auditorium.

"This is so frustrating," Wendy said as we stretched our necks. "I must get closer."

"How close?" I joked.

"I want his autograph," she answered. "I'm not joking."

"Lots of luck."

Wendy doesn't believe in luck. After the concert she dragged me here, to this hotel lobby where we are now sitting. We just sit.

"Are we waiting for him to come into the lobby?" I ask.

"No. He probably got spirited into the hotel through a back or side entrance." Wendy looks at her watch. "He's showered and is relaxing now. He's feeling rested, triumphant and receptive."

"Receptive to what?"

"To meeting us. To autographing *my* album."

"How are you going to accomplish that? You don't actually know that he's staying at this hotel, and even if he is, you don't know his room number."

Wendy stands up. "Don't be so negative, Rosalind. Come," she says.

I follow her to one of those telephones that connect the caller to hotel rooms. She dials a number. She waits. Then she says, "Craig the Cat, please." She looks at me. "I found him! Listen!" She tilts the receiver so that I, too, can hear what's being said. It's a strain, but I can hear.

A woman is on the other end. "How did you find out where Craig the Cat is staying?" she asks. "The leak. I need to know where the leak is."

"There isn't any. I'm the only one with the information. Please be nice. I want his autograph."

"Who doesn't."

"Help me get it, please. What are my chances?"

"Poor to non-existent."

"Oh."

"I'm his manager and, my dear, I'm his mother. I protect Craig from two vantage points. I keep a low profile. Now, how many other fans know where he's staying?"

"None that I know of."

"You mean you didn't peddle the information to the highest bidder?"

"I wouldn't do that."

"Maybe not, dear, but I'm tired of his fans. They tug at Craig's whiskers. They pull his tail. Leave him alone! I'm hanging up."

Click.

Wendy sighs. "We'll just have to wait until he goes into that place over there to eat."

"Haven't you ever heard of room service?"

"Craig doesn't like room service. He doesn't like dining rooms, either. He's a coffee shop person."

"How do you know?"

"I know."

"How did you know his room number?"

"I knew."

"And you knew his mother is his manager?"

"I knew."

We are sitting in the overstuffed chairs again. Wendy is watching and waiting. I see no human-size cat in the lobby. I feel like going to sleep.

Almost an hour goes by. Suddenly, Wendy pokes me.

"It's him! It's him!"

I look up. A guy who seems to be about twenty or twenty-five is passing by with a woman who looks old enough to be his mother. He is lean. She is not. They are dressed normally.

I whisper to Wendy. "*That's* Craig the Cat? How do you know? He looks like an ordinary guy."

Wendy doesn't answer. She stands up and starts to follow the guy and the woman. They are heading for the hotel coffee shop. I follow all of them. I see the guy and the woman sit down. They are looking at menus.

Wendy rushes up to them, clutching her album. "May I have your autograph?" she asks the guy.

The woman glares at Wendy. "He doesn't give autographs," she says. "He's just a civilian. Can't you see he's just a civilian?"

"*You're Craig the Cat!*" Wendy says to the guy.

She says it too loudly.

"How do you know I'm Craig the Cat?" the guy asks. Also too loudly.

People in the coffee shop turn and stare. They repeat, "Craig the Cat!"

Suddenly somebody with a camera materializes and aims the camera at Craig. Wendy bends down and puts her face in front of Craig's. It happens so fast, I can't believe it. The photographer says, "Get out of the way, kid."

Craig's mother glares at the photographer. "Shoo!" she says, waving her hand. "Shoo immediately!"

The photographer leaves. So does Wendy. She runs back to me. I am hiding behind a fern.

Wendy has lost her cool. "Let's get out of here before we're kicked out or arrested," she says.

We rush toward a door.

"Wait!" Someone is yelling at us.

When I hear the word *wait*, it's a signal for me to move even faster. But Wendy stops. "It's *him!*" she says, without turning around.

I turn. It *is* Craig the Cat. He's alone. He rushes up to Wendy. "How did you know me?" he asks. "I didn't tell the media where I was staying. And I certainly didn't give out my room number. I wasn't wearing my cat costume. And I was with my mother. So *how*?"

Wendy looks at me. She's trying to decide if she should answer. Something in her wants to and something in her doesn't want to. She turns back to Craig. "I'm an expert on you," she says. "I know you like fancy, old hotels, and this is the oldest and the fanciest in town. I know your lucky number is twelve, so I figured you'd stay on the twelfth floor in room 1212. I know you always wear red socks when you're not performing. So tonight I watched ankles in the lobby. And I knew you'd be with your manager – your mother."

"What about the photographer?"

"I know you don't want to be photographed without your cat costume. In an interview of October eighth of this year, you said it would wreck your feline image. So when I saw the photographer trying to take your picture, I put my face in front of yours."

"You did that for me?"

"I'd do it for any special friend."

"But you don't know me."

"Yes, I do. When I read about someone, I get to know him. I don't believe everything I read, of course. I pick out certain parts. I look for the reality behind the unreality. I went through seventy-one pages about Craig the Cat, in eleven different magazines, and I ended up thinking of you as my friend."

Craig the Cat is staring at Wendy as if *he's* the fan. He's in awe of *her*! It's nothing very earthshaking. It's not like there's a crowd roaring or it's a summit meeting of world leaders or a momentous change in the universe. It's just a small, nice moment in the lobby of The Dominion Imperial International Hotel, and it will never go away for Wendy.

We're back in the hotel coffee shop. Four of us are sitting around a table, eating. Craig's mother is beaming benevolently like a contented mother cat presiding over her brood, which now includes Wendy and me in addition to Craig. After we finish eating, Wendy hands her record album to Craig. "Now may I have your autograph?" she asks.

Craig pulls out a pen and writes on the album jacket. I hope that Wendy will show me what he writes. Maybe she won't. Whatever she does will be okay, though. Maybe this will be the first private entry in her collection of reality and unreality about her new friend, Craig the Cat.

She's entitled.

As for me, I'm now sitting in a chair in a hotel coffee shop as a new and honoured member of this Clan of the Cat. It has been a strange and kind of wonderful day, thanks to my friend, Wendy the Expert. I'm glad I'm here. If you take away some of the ferns and a few fat chairs and most of the carpeting, The Dominion Imperial International Hotel definitely has possibilities.

DEAR BRUCE SPRINGSTEEN

KEVIN MAJOR

August 14

DEAR BRUCE SPRINGSTEEN
   I hope you don't mind long letters because a lot has happened since this morning.

I'm writing this in the apartment in Callum where Dad (and this woman Charlene) have been living. It's not much of a place. It's small and not in such hot shape. It could use a good cleaning up.

I ended up here tonight, after a long trip and a long time tracking down the old man.

I left the house about ten o'clock this morning. I told Mom I was going over to Sean's and that I wouldn't be home for lunch. All she said was to be sure to be back by three-thirty. She's working evenings and had to be at work by four. I walked around the house and picked up the backpack I had thrown out of my bedroom window. It never had much in it – a change of clothes and my toothbrush and stuff.

Then I walked for about twenty-five minutes, until I got to the highway. It was another hour before anybody picked me up. The guy was only going about ten miles but that was okay. A ride is a ride. He didn't talk much, which suited me fine. It was the second ride that gave me a hell of a fright.

91

I wasn't going to get in with them at first because they looked really dragged out, but I figured I might be stuck where I was forevermore if I started getting choosy. I wasn't in the car two minutes, though, before I realized I was taking a chance I should never have been taking. The old lady would've had a fit if she knew.

There was three of them in an old Mustang, all guys, all of them older than me. Two were maybe twenty, and one fellow looked like he was about sixteen. It was hard to tell. He was crumpled up in the backseat next to me, asleep.

After I got in, the guy who was driving said, "Keep your window down. Pete back there puked up his guts. We scraped him off, but he still stinks. That's what he gets for trying to chug hard liquor." The guy in the passenger seat next to him started to laugh.

I could see it then, dried on his shirt. Enough to make me want to puke myself. I tried to think about something else, but the stink kept bringing me back to it.

The two fellows up front didn't look like they were drunk. Just really dragged out, like I said. The fellow in the passenger seat kept nodding off, then waking up for a few minutes, and then nodding off again. What scared me was thinking that the guy driving might fall asleep, too, and put us off the road. He was driving pretty fast. We might've all ended up dead.

I searched around for a seat belt without giving away what I was doing. I could only find one end. The part it buckled into must have been down between the seats somewhere or under that other guy. I was getting more and more nervous all the time.

The guy that was driving asked me a few questions when I first got aboard, like where I was going and stuff like that, but after he saw that I wasn't much of a talker, he didn't bother with it anymore. Now I started piling the questions to him, not that I wanted to be doing it, but because I figured maybe it would help keep him awake....

What helped me, too, was your music. I got him talking

about you, and once I found out that he really liked certain songs, I had lots to say to keep his mind off driving so fast. I told him all kinds of things about you that he never knew, like how you came to write some of the songs that he liked. I had him convinced he should buy *Nebraska*.

In the end he said, "I like the guy. He's got some real good drivin' music. But I still like Seger better." I'm sure you can handle that.

By then we'd come to a small town about forty miles from Callum. I knew they had to stop for gas. I had my mind made up miles back that I was getting out there. When he hauled up in front of the pumps I said I was going to call a friend of mine who lived there and I was going to his place for a few hours.

The guy said sure, take it easy. When I was getting out of the car I told him again to buy that album. I gave him a fast goodbye and the same to his buddy in the front seat. The guy in the back with the vomit shirt still hadn't moved.

I waited in the phone booth till they had gone off down the highway again, and then I asked the guy pumping gas where the bus to Callum stopped. It wasn't far. It took me about ten minutes to walk there.

I'd made up my mind to take the bus the rest of the way. That ride had freaked me a bit. Why push my luck? It would be a three-hour wait till the right bus came along, but I was in no hurry. I figured I'd rather get where I was going in one piece. I don't hitchhike much. Maybe I need more getting used to it.

The bus ride was just the opposite – really boring. Except that I had all kinds of things on my mind, like was I doing the right thing and was Mom getting worried yet and what do I do if I can't get in touch with the old man? Pretty depressing stuff till I made up my mind that there was no other way and turning back would only make it worse.

When the bus got into the station I went straight to a pay phone and dug through the book till I found BJ's. I wasn't

93

looking for the phone number, just the name of the street it was on.

I went out in front of the station, looked up the street in one direction and then the other, and wondered what I should do. I started to walk toward the part of the city that looked like it had the most traffic. After a while I wised up and asked someone for directions.

It was almost an hour before I finally got in sight of the club. The last part of the walk took me past half a dozen restaurants and fast-food joints. I gave in to breaking another five-dollar bill and bought myself some fries. They kept me from having to go into BJ's right away. I figured I needed a few minutes to gear myself up for that.

Just inside the front door was a sign that said "No Minors Allowed." I never paid it no attention. It was really black inside, I guess because I just came out of the sunlight. The only real light was over the bar and in the corner where the pool tables were. There weren't many people around, a couple of guys shooting pool and a few more standing up around the bar. I gave my eyes a minute or so to get used to it, and then I strolled past all the empty tables to the bar.

The bartender looked at me like I'd better have a good excuse for being there. Before he had a chance to chew me out I asked to see the manager. He said the manager wasn't there. So I told him who I was looking for and asked him if he knew where I could find him. By now everyone in the place was staring at me.

"He's my father."

"Yeah." The bartender raised his eyebrows and stuck out his lower lip. "You're sure?"

I waited, without answering such a stupid question.

"The guy knows his own father, Tom," one of the fellows standing at the bar said.

"Where can I find him?" I asked again.

"He lives in Birchwood Apartments. Which one, I don't know."

I didn't wait around. I got out of there while I was ahead of the game.

Back out in the sunshine, I stopped three people before I found someone who could tell me how to get there.

Lucky it wasn't too far away. It took twenty minutes. None of what I'd been doing all day seemed real until I saw the apartment building. Then it hit me – this is it. All the things I'd practised in my mind that I wanted to say to him came rushing at me, screwing up my head and making me nervous. I shouldn't have been nervous about my own father.

The apartment building is not much to look at from the outside. It needs a paint job real bad. And it could do with a lawn and a few trees. I could tell from the lobby that the inside wasn't going to be any better.

I waited in the lobby till someone came around. There were names on some of the mailboxes but none with the old man's name. 106 had "Charlene Symonds" on it. A woman came in from a taxi with a load of groceries. I opened the outside door for her. While she was searching her purse for a key, I asked her if she knew what apartment he lived in. She told me the basement, 106 she thought it was. I told her he was my father, and when I walked through the open door behind her, she never said nothing.

There was nothing to do, only go to the apartment and ring the buzzer. When I got there, I pressed it twice. I knew it rang inside because I could hear it. I knocked, and there was still no answer. I looked at my watch. It was almost seven-thirty. I sat on the floor with my back against the wall and waited. Every time I heard anyone walking my way, I stood up.

It was more than an hour before I saw him coming. He was wearing the same baseball cap he always wore. New jeans, but the same Budweiser belt buckle. There was a woman walking a half-step behind him.

I looked away as he got closer. He didn't really notice

who I was till he was almost to the door.

"Terry," he said. "My good God!"

He put one arm around my shoulder and pulled me in tight to him.

"Where in the world did you come from?"

All I could do was smile. I didn't know how to say it.

"You've grown. You're taller. Hell, man, it's real good to see ya!"

"Good to see you."

He was waiting for more. I shrugged, relieved, I guess, by all the fuss he made about me.

"Well then, grab your knapsack, come on in," he said as he turned to unlock the door. "This is Charlene," he said. I guess she figured out who I was.

"Excuse the mess," she said.

The place was pretty grungy. Still is. It looks like it hasn't been cleared away for weeks.

The old man, of course, wanted to know all about how I got there. When he found out that Mom didn't know anything about it, he called home and told her where I was. He wanted me to talk to her, but I wouldn't. I knew she'd be calling back before long. Tomorrow probably, knowing Mom. And by then she'd be calmed down, maybe.

He was starved for news. I sat in the living room, and we talked and talked for a long time. Until Charlene came out of the bathroom all dressed up and told him what time it was. He had to get ready. He's in a band, like I figured, and they're playing tonight. He walked down the hall to the bedroom, and Charlene went back into the bathroom again, leaving me to sit around and size things up a bit more.

Dad came out in a rush and said he was sorry for having to run off after me only just getting there. I told him I understood. He said he was sorry that I couldn't come too. He told me I should be able to find some grub in the fridge. When they were going out the door he looked at me and said, "Glad you still think about your old man."

So now I'm here in the apartment writing this letter. Good thing I brought some writing paper of my own. No chance of finding any here.

I'm still hungry. I found some bread and made some toast and had a cup of coffee with it. But that was about all I came across in the house that I was willing to face. Oh yeah, and one of those small cans of fruit cocktail. What was in the fridge was a lost cause – left over and dried out. They must eat out a lot, if you can go by all the plastic forks and packs of salt I see lying around.

That's not all that's lying around. A roach in an ashtray. Rolling papers. I'm sure they must smoke up. Not that I care. I guess I'm a bit surprised at the old man doing it, that's all.

Know something? Basement apartments give me the creeps. I don't know why he'd want to live here. One thing for sure, Mom'd never be able to put up with it. That's something that used to bug the old man – the way everything back home had to be so tidy all the time. All the same, I can't see him getting off on this place.

Anyway, it's getting late, and I'm really tired, and I've

gone a little crazy writing down so much. Man, this letter is going to weigh a ton. I hope it don't sound like I was running off at the mouth. If it does, sorry about that. I didn't make any of it up. That's just the way it happened.

I'm going to stretch out on the couch now and take a nap until they get back.

I don't want to end this off sounding like I'm sorry for coming. I'm not. It's great to see the old man. I didn't know what to expect, and now I know. That's all. I'll get it straight after a while.

Take it easy,
Terry

P.S. It's the next day. (I know this letter is a pretty gross size like it is, but I want to add on this part. Now I got to make out a new envelope.)

I heard them when they got home last night. You couldn't help but hear them. They were both laughing outside the apartment door. It woke me up, but I pretended I was still asleep. Charlene sounded real crazy – she was laughing about something and couldn't stop. They came inside and everything was quiet for a while.

She went down the hall to the bedroom, and he walked over to the couch and stood up by me. He stayed there for the longest time. I didn't move. Then he went away and came back with a blanket and threw it over me. After a while he turned out the light and walked down the hall. I could hear the door to the bedroom close. Charlene started laughing again. I couldn't get back to sleep for a long time.

REVERDY

JESSAMYN WEST

I NEVER SEE ASTERS without remembering her, never the haze of their pink and lavender blossoming as summer dies, but her name is in my heart: Reverdy, Reverdy.

I never say her name – not to anyone. When people ask about her, as they do occasionally even now, I say "she" and "her". "She is still gone." "We do not hear from her." "Yes, she was very beautiful," I say. But not her name.

Not Reverdy. That is buried deep, deep in my heart. Where the blood is warmest and thickest . . . where it has a sound to me like bells, or water running, or the doves whose voices in the evening wind are like smoke among the madrones and eucalyptus.

I have longed all these years to tell her how it was the night she left. You may scarcely believe it, but it is worse to have a good thing that is not true believed about you, than a bad. To be thanked for an act you meant to be harmful – every year those words sharpen until at last they cut like knives.

You mustn't think she was like me. She wasn't in the least. Not inside or out. She had dark hair like a cloud. Yes

99

really. It wasn't curly, but it didn't hang straight. It billowed out. And her face – oh, you mustn't think it was anything like mine. She had hazel eyes and a pointed chin. And you've seen lots of people, haven't you, with very live, animated faces and dead eyes? It was just the other way with Reverdy. Her face was always quiet, but her eyes were so alive they glowed. Oh, she was the most beautiful, most alive, and most loved girl in the world, and she was my sister.

I cannot bear for people to say we were alike. She was really good, and I was just a show-off.

Mother – she was better later, and gentler, but then she was bad, cruel and suspicious with Reverdy. Everybody loved Reverdy. Not just the boys. But Mother wouldn't see that. She always acted as if Reverdy were boy-crazy, as if Reverdy tried to entice the boys to her. But it wasn't true. Reverdy never lifted a finger to a boy, though they were around her all the time from the day she was ten. Bringing her May baskets, or valentines, or ponies to ride.

And the big, tough boys liked her, too. When she was twelve and thirteen, big eighteen-year-olds would come over and sit on the steps and smoke and talk to Reverdy. They never said anything out of the way. I know because most of the time I was with them. Reverdy didn't care. She never wanted to be alone with them. Reverdy would listen to them until she got tired, then she'd say, "Goodbye for now." She'd always say, "Goodbye for now," and then she'd go out and play – maybe "Run, sheep, run" – with the little kids my age. And the little kids would all shout when Reverdy came out to play with them. If the game had been about to die, it would come to life again. If some of the kids had gone home, they'd yell, "Hey, Johnnie" or "Hey, Mary," or whoever it was, "Reverdy's going to play," and then everyone would come back, and in a minute or two the game would be better than ever.

I used to be awfully proud of being her sister. I don't know what I would have done without her. I was a terribly plain little frump – I wore glasses and had freckles. If I hadn't been Reverdy's sister, I'd have had to sit and play jacks by myself, until Joe came along. But boys would try to get Reverdy's attention by doing things for me. They'd say to her, "Does your sister want to ride on my handlebars?" And Reverdy would say, all glowing, happier than if she'd been asked, "Do you, Sister?" Of course I did, and when the boy came back, she'd ride with him just to thank him.

I don't know why people, why the boys, liked her so. Of course, she was beautiful, but I think it was more that she was so much – well, whatever she was at the moment; she never pretended. She talked with people when she wanted to, and when she got tired of them, she didn't stay on pretending, but said, "Goodbye for now," and left.

But Mother would never believe she wasn't boy-crazy, and I would hear her talking to Reverdy about girls who got in trouble, and how she'd rather see a daughter of hers in her grave. I didn't know what she was talking about, but it would make my face burn and scalp tingle just to hear her. She wouldn't talk sorrowfully or lovingly to Reverdy, but with hate. It wasn't Reverdy she hated, but you couldn't tell that, looking at her. She would bend over Reverdy and shake her finger and there would be long ugly lines from her nose to her mouth, and her eyebrows would be drawn down until you could see the bony ridges they were supposed to cover, all bare and hard. It used to make me tremble to see her. Then Reverdy would get mad. I don't think she knew half the time what Mother was talking about, either – only that Mother was full of hate and suspicion. She'd wait until Mother had finished, then she'd go to the foothills for a walk, even if it was dark, and stay for a long time. And then Mother would think she was out with some boy again.

I remember one time my mother came to me and said, "Clare, I want you to tiptoe out to the arbour and see what's going on there. Reverdy's out there with Sam Foss,

and I haven't heard a sound out of them for an hour or more."

The arbour was a kind of little bower covered with honeysuckle. There was only a tiny little door, and the honeysuckle strands hung so thick over it the arbour was a kind of dark, sweet-smelling cave. Reverdy and I used to play house there. I knew I ought to say I wouldn't go spying on Reverdy, but I wanted to please Mother, so I went creeping out towards the arbour, holding my breath, walking on my toes. I didn't know then – but I've found out since – you can't do a thing without becoming that thing. When I started out to look for Reverdy I was her little sister, loving her. But creeping that way, holding my breath, spying, I became a spy. My hands got heavy and hot and my mouth dry, and I wanted to see her doing . . . whatever it was Mother was fearful of.

And then when I got to the arbour and peeped in, I saw

that Chummie, our ten-year-old brother, was there with them, and they were all practising sign language. Deaf-and-dumb language was the rage with kids that summer, and there was that big Sam Foss sitting cross-legged, practising sign language so hard he was sweating. They had oranges rolled until they were soft, and straws stuck in them to suck the juice out.

That's all they were doing. Practising deaf-and-dumb language, and sucking oranges that way, playing they were bottles of pop. I guess they'd taken a vow not to talk, because nobody said a word. Even when Reverdy saw me peeping in, she didn't say anything, just spelled out, "Hello, Sister." But my hands felt so hot and swollen I couldn't spell a thing, and I just stood there and stared until I heard Mother call me to her, where she was standing strained and waiting on the back steps.

"They're playing sign language with Chummie," I told her.

"Is Chummie with them?" she asked, and her face relaxed and had a sort of shamed look on it, I thought.

I went in the house and put on the old dress I went swimming in, and floated around in the irrigation canal until supper was over, so I wouldn't have to sit and look across the table at Reverdy.

Things like that were always happening. I loved Reverdy more than anybody, and I hated Mother sometimes for spying and suspecting and lecturing. But I wanted people to love me. And especially you want your mother to love you – isn't that true? And no one loved me the way Reverdy was loved. I wasn't beautiful and spontaneous, I had to work hard and do good deeds to be loved. I couldn't be free the way Reverdy was. I was always thinking of the effect I was making. I couldn't say, "Goodbye for now," and let people go to hell if they didn't like me. I was afraid they'd never come back, and I'd be left . . . alone. But Reverdy didn't care. She liked being alone – and that's the reason people loved her, I guess.

One evening in October, when it was almost dark, I was coming home from the library, coasting across lots in the hot dry Santa Ana that had been blowing all day. Cool weather had already come, and then three days of this hot wind. Dust everywhere. Under your eyelids, between your fingers, in your mouth. When we went to school in the morning the first thing we'd do would be to write our names in the dust on our desks. I had on a skirt full of pleats that evening, and I pulled the pleats out wide so the skirt made a sort of sail and the wind almost pushed me along. I watched the tumbleweeds blowing, and listened to the wind in the clump of eucalyptus by the barn, and felt miserable and gritty. Then I saw Reverdy walking up and down the driveway by the house, and I felt suddenly glad. Reverdy loved the wind, even Santa Ana's, and she was always out walking or running when the wind blew, if she didn't have any work to do. She liked to carry a scarf in her hand and hold it up in the wind so she could feel it tug and snap. When I saw Reverdy, I forgot how dusty and hot the wind was and remembered only how alive it was and how Reverdy loved it. I ran towards her, but she didn't wave or say a word, and when she reached the end of the driveway she turned her back on me and started walking towards the barn.

Before I had a chance to say a word to her, Mother came to the door and called to me to come in and not to talk to Reverdy. As soon as I heard her voice, before I could see her face, I knew there was some trouble – some trouble with Reverdy – and I knew what kind of trouble, too. I went in the house and shut the door. The sound of Reverdy's footsteps on the pepper leaves in the driveway outside stopped, and Mother put her head out the window and said, "You're to keep walking, Reverdy, and not stop. Understand? I want to hear footsteps and I want them to be brisk." Then she closed the window, though it was hard to do against the wind.

I stood with my face to the window and looked out into

the dusty, windy dark where I could just see Reverdy in her white dress walking up and down, never stopping, her head bent, not paying any attention to the wind she loved. It made me feel sick to see her walking up and down there in the dusty dark like a homeless dog, while we were snug inside.

But Mother came over to the window and took the curtain out of my hand and put it back over the glass. Then she put her arm around my shoulders and pressed me close to her and said, "Mother's own dear girl who has never given her a moment's trouble."

That wasn't true. Mother had plenty of fault to find with me usually – but it was sweet to have her speak lovingly to me, to be cherished and appreciated. Maybe you can't

understand that, maybe your family was always loving, maybe you were always dear little daughter, or maybe a big golden wonder-boy. But not me and not my mother. So try to understand how it was with me then, and how happy it made me to have Mother put her arms around me. Yes, I thought, I'm mother's comfort. And I forgot I couldn't make a boy look at me if I wanted to, and blamed Reverdy for not being able to steer clear of them the way I did. She just hasn't any consideration for any of us, I decided. Oh, I battened on Reverdy's downfall all right.

Then Father and Chummie came in, and Mother took Father away to the kitchen and talked to him there in a fast, breathless voice. I couldn't hear what she was saying, but I knew what she was talking about, of course. Chummie and I sat there in the dark. He whirled first one way and then another on the piano stool.

"What's Reverdy doing walking up and down outside there?" he asked.

"She's done something bad again," I told him.

Mother's voice got higher and higher, and Chummie said he'd have to go feed his rabbits, and I was left alone in the dark listening to her, and to Reverdy's footsteps on the pepper leaves. I decided to light the lights, but when I did – we had acetylene lights – the blue-white glare was so terrible I couldn't stand it. Not to sit alone in all that light and look at the dusty room and listen to the dry sound of the wind in the palms outside, and see Reverdy's books on the library table where she'd put them when she got home from school, with a big bunch of wilted asters laid across them. Reverdy always kept her room filled with flowers, and if she couldn't get flowers, she'd have leaves or grasses.

No, I couldn't stand that, so I turned out the lights and sat in the dark and listened to Reverdy's steps, not fast or light now, but heavy and slow – and I sat there and thought I was Mother's comforter, not causing her trouble like Reverdy.

Pretty soon I heard Mother and Father go outside, and then their voices beneath the window. Father was good, and he was for reason, but with Mother he lost his reason. He was just like me, I guess. He wanted Mother to love him, and because he did he would go out and say to Reverdy the things Mother wanted him to say.

Chummie came back from feeding his rabbits and sat with me in the dark room. Then I got the idea of a way to show Mother how much I was her comfort and mainstay, her darling younger daughter, dutiful and harmonious as hell. Mother wanted me and Chummie to be musical – she'd given up with Reverdy – but Chummie and I had taken lessons for years. Usually we kicked and howled at having to play; so I thought, If we play now, it will show Mother how thoughtful and reliable we are. It will cheer her up while she's out there in the wind talking to that bad Reverdy. Yes, she will think, I have one fine, dependable daughter anyway.

So I said to Chummie, "Let's play something for Mother." So he got out his violin, and we played that piece I've ever afterwards hated. Over and over again, just as sweet as we could make it. Oh, I felt smug as hell as I played. I sat there on the piano stool with feet just so, and my hands just so, and played carefully, every note saying, "Mother's comfort. Mother's comfort. Played by her good, fine, reliable daughter."

We could hear Mother's high voice outside the window and Reverdy's low murmur now and then. Chummie finally got tired of playing – the music wasn't saying anything to him – and went out to the kitchen to get something to eat. I went too, but the minute I took a bite I knew I wasn't hungry, and Chummie and I both went to bed. I lay in bed a long time waiting to hear Mother and Reverdy come in, but there wasn't any sound but the wind.

I was asleep when Reverdy did come in. She sat down on the side of my bed, and it was just her sitting there that

finally woke me. Then, when I was awake, she picked up my hand and began to press my fingertips one by one, and spoke in the sweetest, kindest voice. You'd never have thought to hear her that she had just spent four or five hours the way she did.

She said, "I'll never forget your playing for me, Sister. Never. Never. It was kind and beautiful of you. Just when I thought I was all alone, I heard you telling me not to be sad." Then she leaned over and kissed me and said, "Good night, now. I've put some asters in water for you. They're a little wilted but I think they'll be all right by morning. Go to sleep, now. I'll never forget, Clare."

If I could only have told her, if I could only have told her then. If I could have said to her, "I was playing for Mother, Reverdy. I guess I was jealous of your always having the limelight. I wanted to be first for once." If I could only have said, "I love you more that anything, Reverdy, but I have a mean soul," she would have put her cheek to mine and said, "Oh, Clare, what a thing to say."

But I couldn't do it, and next morning she was gone. And there on the table by my bed were the asters she had left for me, grown fresh overnight.

THE CEMENT TRUCK

LAURENCE LASKY

I RECALL BEING ON THE BUS, wishing my shoulder was separated, or that my right arm had been plastered to a cast and the cast had a dozen names written on it. "Mr Kanele," I wanted to say but didn't dare to, "my left ankle is busted," or, "Mr Kanele, I can't move my right leg." A new thought sprang into my mind. I would arrive at that school, walk up to the nearest wall, and bang my head against it ten or twelve times. This way I would at least sustain a concussion or a brain tumour. Or maybe I could bend my little finger back to my wrist. He wouldn't send a guy out onto the mat with nine fingers. Yes, he would. He would send a one-legged third grader onto the mat if he was presented with the choice of that or a forfeit. "Where's Scutter, my eighty-six-pound protégé? Hey, Scutter, want to wrestle varsity today?" I could picture him sitting smugly in his English class with his legs tied up in a square knot and with four fingers stuck in his mouth. Nope, it would be against him, me against the world. Maybe I could slash my wrists or slit my throat. That wouldn't work. Nothing would work. Kanele wouldn't accept any excuse I proposed to him.

Why was I the only guy on the bus changing from rock to petrified wood? All the rest of the hearty wrestlers were talking or singing or acting funny or being perfectly gay. How do you account for that? Maybe all wrestlers are idiots. In fact, you have to be an idiot if you're a wrestler. Everybody hates wrestling. Therefore, all wrestlers are idiots. Including me, for being on this ridiculous team.

"There it is, to the left," said one of the wrestlers.

"Yep, that's South Rock, all right."

I pressed my nose against the window. There it was, ugly and cruel. The bus continued rumbling along, but now I felt each bump kicking my stomach so I could hear it bouncing emptily like a tin can.

Kanele had told me about the guy I was to wrestle. "He's a county champ, Lasky. A slicker wrestler doesn't exist. He knows every single move in the book. Strong, too. Strong as a bull. You're in for one, Lasky."

That really encouraged me. We would walk into that school, and there he would be. I'd walk up to him and he'd look at me and say, "You know what? You're the sickliest little thing I've ever wrestled. I eat guys like you for breakfast." Just swell. And I would laugh, heh, heh, and say back to him, "Are you on weight? What's your record? Did Yates beat you? Don't you think wrestling is a silly sport? I hate wrestling. Too much callisthenics. I'm going to be a doctor when I grow up." Then he would look at me as if I were a bug. He would shrug his shoulders and said, "That's your problem, buddy." I would watch him stalking off.

By now we were inside the building. Ed Reynolds said, "Hey, some joint here!" Wrestlers must be perfect morons. No one will be able to drag me to that wrestling room next year.

Then Kanele walked up to me. It was rumoured that Mr Kanele was the runner-up in the 123-pound division in the Panama games in 1954. He had a peppery walk, like some bowlegged sailor, and he came up to me and slapped me

111

on the shoulders. "Get ready. Strip down. The weigh-in's in twenty minutes."

I always associated the phrase "weigh-in" with World War Three or Edgar Allan Poe on a chilly December night.

"I thought you said the weigh-in wouldn't be till four?"

"My, you really *are* anxious, Lasky," he said, slapping me on the shoulder.

At wrestling weigh-ins, everybody parades up to the scale nude and one by one they hop on the scale, some keeping their heels off it, some exhaling air furiously, others trying to amputate some useless part of the body. For most of them it boiled down to their heads. Wrestlers are all morons.

County champ was on weight. I was on weight. I wished I wasn't.

He wasn't too over-confident when he stepped on the scale. He hopped on singing, "Row, row, row your boat." Boy, that made me mad. "Buddy," I murmured to myself, "I'm going to beat the daylights out of you." Yes, I was going to beat the daylights out of him. Before twenty million cheering fans. I was going to get him on the mat, whip him into a double-knee-drop leg breaker, and win the gold belt. Everybody would be cheering like crazy. And Kanele would walk up to me and say, "You did it, Lasky, you did it!" And I would say, "I couldn't have done it without you, Mr Kanele." Then I would be mobbed by a hungry band of autograph seekers and twenty or thirty photographers. Cameras flashing everywhere.

Just before the match, Kanele gave us his usual pep talk. He wasn't one of those I-don't-care-whether-you-win-or-lose-boys-it's-how-you-play-the-game men.

"Listen, you guys. We've lost nine matches in a row. It's about time we saved a bit of our school's honour. Lasky, you start us off. Give the boys a lift by pinning the county champ. Now come on, run out onto that mat."

See, I was going to pin the county champ.

We went out onto the mat, all of us trying to look

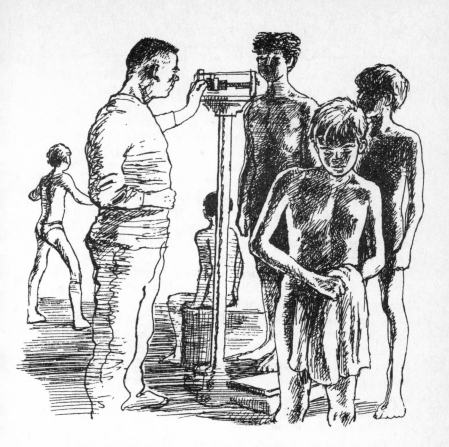

complicated and important. We looked like a pack of firemen. I felt stupid.

I remember the mat being soft and squishy. While everybody else was deciding what hold to pull, or what reversals to try, or how they were going to take their man down, I was thinking how nice and soft the mat was. I was also thinking how sick I was. Sick of Kanele, sick of wrestling, sick of all the idiot wrestlers around me, and sick of worry.

"Listen," I said to myself, "the worst thing that can happen to you is that you'll get pinned in the first period. So what? What's so terrible about getting pinned in the

113

first period? It's been done before. Every member of this team has been pinned in the first period before. Almost every member."

We sat down in our places and then they came running out onto the mat. The crowd was unlike our crowds. At home matches, we were accustomed to eight people looking down from our side, and two of them were managers, one was a cheerleader (the one who had drawn the smallest ballot), and two were janitors. Here there were a thousand screaming idiots, all of them completely out of their minds. Everybody was clapping their hands. This I remember. I also remember myself saying, "I got to get out of here."

"Victory! Victory! Victory! Kill these guys! Smash them! Break them! Maul them! Beat the hell out of these guys! Stomp them into the ground."

All this time I remained perfectly frigid and the rest of the idiots around me weren't perfectly gay any more.

I was now standing in my corner, Kanele talking to me, and the county champ was standing in his corner, his manager talking to him. "Mr Kanele, I think my back is brok—"

"What's that, Lasky?"

"Nothing, oh, nothing."

The match is a blurred picture. They always are. I remember going out there and shaking hands with the guy and giving him a pleasant smile which he didn't see and the moron referee tooting his whistle and that monster walking towards me and myself saying to myself, "Oh, hell!"

Thwap. I was on the mat. He was on me like an octopus. He had my arm, and the other arm. Now the leg and then my head. Then the other leg. Then my nose was pushed into that soft, squishy mat. It was blue-green. The one at the other school was white, but I liked this one better. It was a pretty blue-green. All soft and squishy. You would have liked to step on it; your foot would have sunk in three inches. I wished I could have been rolled up in it and sent bouncing down a hill. On a cool, windy day in April. With swaying trees all around and a little brook at my side.

Then I felt a cement truck on my chest. The referee's hand came down and his whistle blew. But the crowd wasn't there. I looked at Kanele. Kanele looked at me. Agony, agony, agony.

Here it came, the deadly ray gun. His eyebrows were down, his mouth expressionless. I could detect just that little twitch of the upper lip he was so good at. The eyes were fixed, fixed on my eyes. I couldn't avoid them. It was terrible.

"Well, Lasky," said Kanele, "at least you didn't quit." He lied. Boy, did he lie.

THE EVACUEES

NINA BAWDEN

from Carrie's War

Carrie and Nick, along with many other children, have been evacuated from London because of the war. They are on their way to a small town in Wales.

HE THREW UP all over Miss Fazackerly's skirt. He had been feeling sick ever since they left the main junction and climbed into the joggling, jolting little train for the last lap of their journey, but the sudden whistle had finished him.

Such a noise – it seemed to split the sky open. "Enough to frighten the dead," Miss Fazackerly said, mopping her skirt and Nick's face with her handkerchief. He lay back limp as a rag and let her do it, the way he always let people do things for him, not lifting a finger. "Poor lamb," Miss Fazackerly said, but Carrie looked stern.

"It's all his own fault. He's been stuffing his face ever since we left London. Greedy pig. Dustbin."

116

He had not only eaten his own packed lunch – sandwiches and cold sausages and bananas – but most of Carrie's as well. She had let him have it to comfort him because he minded leaving home and their mother more than she did. Or had looked as if he minded more. She thought now that it was just one of his acts, put on to get sympathy. Sympathy and chocolate! He had had all her chocolate, too! "I knew he'd be sick," she said smugly.

"Might have warned me then, mightn't you?" Miss Fazackerly said. Not unkindly, she was one of the kindest teachers in the school, but Carrie wanted to cry suddenly. If she had been Nick she would have cried, or at least put on a hurt face. Being Carrie she stared crossly out of the carriage window at the big mountain on the far side of the valley. It was brown and purple on the top and green lower down; streaked with silver trickles of water and dotted with sheep.

Sheep and mountains. "Oh, it'll be such fun," their mother had said when she kissed them goodbye at the station. "Living in the country instead of the stuffy old city. You'll love it, you see if you don't!" As if Hitler had arranged this old war for their benefit, just so that Carrie and Nick could be sent away in a train with gas masks slung over their shoulders and their names on cards round their necks. Labelled like parcels – Caroline Wendy Willow and Nicholas Peter Willow – only with no address to be sent to. None of them, not even the teachers, knew where they were going. "That's part of the adventure," Carrie's mother had said, and not just to cheer them up; it was her nature to look on the bright side. If she found herself in hell, Carrie thought now, she'd just say, "Well, at least we'll be *warm*."

Thinking of her mother, always making the best of things (or pretending to: when the train began to move she had stopped smiling) Carrie nearly did cry. There was a lump like a pill stuck in her throat. She swallowed hard and pulled faces.

117

The train was slowing. "Here we are," Miss Fazackerly said. "Collect your things, don't leave anything. Take care of Nick, Carrie."

Carrie scowled. She loved Nick, loved him so much sometimes that it gave her a pain, but she hated to be told to do something she was going to do anyway. And she was bored with Nick at the moment. That dying-duck look as he struggled to get his case down from the rack! "Leave it to me, silly baby," she said, jumping up on the seat. Dust flew and he screwed up his face. "You're making me sneeze," he complained. "Don't *bounce*, Carrie."

They all seemed to have more luggage than when they had started. Suitcases that had once been quite light now felt as if they were weighed down with stones – and got heavier as they left the small station and straggled down a steep, cinder path. Carrie had Nick's case as well as her own and a carrier bag with a broken string handle. She tucked it under one arm but it kept slipping backwards and her gas mask banged her knee as she walked.

"Someone help Caroline, please," Miss Fazackerly cried, rushing up and down the line of children like a sheep dog. Someone did – Carrie felt the carrier bag go from under her arm, then one suitcase.

It was a bigger boy. Carrie blushed, but he wasn't a Senior: he wore a cap like all the boys under sixteen, and although he was tall, he didn't look very much older than she was. She glanced sideways and said, "Thank you *so* much," in a grown-up voice like her mother's.

He grinned shyly back. He had steel-rimmed spectacles, a few spots on his chin. He said, "Well, I suppose this is what they call our ultimate destination. Not much of a place, is it?"

They were off the cinder track now, walking down a hilly street where small, dark houses opened straight on to the pavement. There was sun on the mountain above them, but the town was in shadow; the air struck chill on their cheeks and smelled dusty.

"Bound to be dirty," Carrie said. "A coal-mining town."

"I didn't mean dirt. Just that it's not big enough to have a good public library."

It seemed a funny thing to bother about at the moment. Carrie said, "The first place was bigger. Where we stopped at the junction." She peered at his label and read his name. Albert Sandwich. She said, "If you came earlier on in the alphabet you could have stayed there. You only just missed it, they divided us after the R's. Do your friends call you Ally, or Bert?"

119

"I don't care for my name to be abbreviated," he said. "Nor do I like being called Jam, or Jelly, or even Peanut Butter."

He spoke firmly but Carrie thought he looked anxious.

"I hadn't thought of sandwiches," she said. "Only of the town Sandwich in Kent, because my granny lives there. Though my dad says she'll have to move now in case the Germans land on the coast." She thought of the Germans landing and her grandmother running away with her things on a cart like a refugee in a newspaper picture. She gave a loud, silly laugh and said, "If they did, my gran 'ud give them What For. She's not frightened of anyone, I bet she could even stop Hitler. Go up on her roof and pour boiling oil down!"

Albert looked at her, frowning. "I doubt if that would be very helpful. Old people aren't much use in a war. Like kids – best out of the way."

His grave tone made Carrie feel foolish. She wanted to say it was only a joke, about boiling oil, but they had arrived at a building with several steps leading up and were told to get into single file so that their names could be checked at the door. Nick was waiting there, holding Miss Fazackerly's hand. She said, "There you are, darling. There she is, didn't I tell you?" And to Carrie, "Don't lose him again!"

She ticked them off on her list, saying aloud, "Two Willows, one Sandwich."

Nick clung to Carrie's sleeve as they went through the door into a long, dark room with pointed windows. It was crowded and noisy. Someone said to Carrie, "Would you like a cup of tea, bach? And a bit of cake, now?" She was a cheerful, plump woman with a sing-song Welsh voice. Carrie shook her head; she felt cake would choke her. "Stand by there, then," the woman said. "There by the wall with the others, and someone will choose you."

Carrie looked round, bewildered, and saw Albert Sandwich. She whispered, "What's happening?" and he said, "A kind of cattle auction, it seems."

He sounded calmly disgusted. He gave Carrie her suitcase, then marched to the end of the hall, sat down on his own, and took a book out of his pocket.

Carrie wished she could do that. Sit down and read as if nothing else mattered. But she had already begun to feel ill with shame at the fear that no one would choose her, the way she always felt when they picked teams at school. Suppose she was left to the last! She dragged Nick into the line of waiting children and stood, eyes on the ground, hardly daring to breathe. When someone called out, "A nice little girl for Mrs Davies, now," she felt she would suffocate. She looked up but unfocused her eyes so that passing faces blurred and swam in front of her.

Nick's hand tightened in hers. She looked at his white face and the traces of sick round his mouth and wanted to shake him. No one would take home a boy who looked like that, so pale and delicate. They would think he was bound to get ill and be a trouble to them. She said in a low, fierce voice, "Why don't you smile and look nice," and he blinked with surprise, looking so small and so sweet that she softened. She said, "Oh, it's all right, I'm not cross. I won't leave you."

Minutes passed, feeling like hours. Children left the line and were taken away. Only unwanted ones left, Carrie thought. She and Nick, and a few tough-looking boys, and an ugly girl with a squint who had two little sisters. And Albert Sandwich who was still sitting quietly on his suitcase, reading his book and taking no notice. *He* didn't care! Carrie tossed her head and hummed under her breath to show she didn't either.

Someone had stopped in front of her. Someone said, "Surely you can take two, Miss Evans?"

"Two girls, perhaps. Not a boy and a girl, I'm afraid. I've only the one room, see, and my brother's particular."

Particular about what, Carrie wondered. But Miss Evans looked nice; a little like a red squirrel Carrie had once seen,

121

peering round a tree in a park. Reddish brown hair and bright, button eyes, and a shy, quivering look.

Carrie said, "Nick sleeps in my room at home because he has bad dreams sometimes. I always look after him and he's no trouble at all."

Miss Evans looked doubtful. "Well, I don't know what my brother will say. Perhaps I can chance it." She smiled at Carrie. "There's pretty eyes you have, girl! Like green glass!"

Carrie smiled back. People didn't often notice her when Nick was around. *His* eyes were dark blue, like their mother's. She said, "Oh, Nick's the pretty one, really."

Miss Evans walked fast. She was a little woman, not much taller than Carrie, but seemed strong as a railway porter, carrying their cases as if they weighed nothing. Out of the hall, down the street. They stopped outside a grocery shop with the name SAMUEL ISAAC EVANS above the door and Miss Evans took a key from her bag. She said, "There's a back way and you'll use that, of course, but we'll go through the front for the once, as my brother's not here."

The shop was dim and smelled mustily pleasant. Candles and tarred kindling, and spices, Carrie thought, wrinkling her nose. A door at the back led into a small room with a huge desk almost filling it. "My brother's office," Miss Evans said in a hushed voice and hurried them through into a narrow, dark hall with closed doors and a stair rising up. It was darker here than the shop and there was a strong smell of polish.

Polished linoleum, a shining-glass sea, with rugs scattered like islands. Not a speck of dust anywhere. Miss Evans looked down at their feet. "Better change into your slippers before we go up to your bedroom."

"We haven't got any," Carrie said. She meant to explain that there hadn't been room in their cases but before she could speak Miss Evans turned bright red and said quickly, "Oh, I'm so sorry, how silly of me, why should you?

Never mind, as long as you're careful and tread on the drugget.''

A strip of white cloth covered the middle of the stair carpet. They trod on this as they climbed; looking back from the top, Carrie saw the marks of their rubber-soled shoes and felt guilty, though it wasn't her fault. Nick whispered, ''She thinks we're poor children, too poor to have slippers,'' and giggled.

Carrie supposed he was right. Nick was good at guessing what people were thinking. But she didn't feel like giggling; everywhere was so tidy and clean it made her despair. She thought she would never dare touch anything in this house in case she left marks. She wouldn't dare *breathe* – even her breath might be dirty!

Miss Evans was looking at Nick. ''What did you say,

dear?" she asked, but didn't wait for an answer. "Here's the bathroom," she said – proudly, it seemed. "Hot and cold running water, *and* a flush toilet. And your room, just by here."

It was a small room with two narrow beds and a hooked rug between them. A wardrobe and a wicker chair and a large, framed notice on the wall. The black letters said, The Eye Of The Lord Is Upon You.

Miss Evans saw Carrie looking at this. She said, "My brother is very strong Chapel. So you'll have to be especially good, Sundays. No games or books, see? Except the Bible, of course."

The children stared at her. She smiled shyly. "It may not be what you're used to but it's better to get things straight from the start, isn't it? Mr Evans is a good man, but strict. Manners and tidiness and keeping things clean. He says dirt and sloppy habits are an insult to the Lord. So you will be good, won't you? You look like good children."

It was almost as if she were pleading with them. Asking them to be good so that *she* wouldn't get into trouble. Carrie was sorry for her, though she felt very uncomfortable. Neither she nor Nick were particularly tidy: at home, in their warm, muddly house, no one had expected them to be. Milly, their maid, always picked up their toys and made their beds and put their clothes away. Carrie said, "We'll try to be good, Miss Evans."

"Call me Auntie," Miss Evans said, "Auntie Louise. Or Auntie Lou, if that's easier. But you'd best call my brother Mr Evans. You see, he's a Councillor." She paused and then went on in the same proud tone she had used when she showed them the bathroom. "Mr Evans is a very important man. He's at a Council meeting just now. I think I'd best give you your supper before he comes back, hadn't I?"

CATALOGUE CATS

ANN CAMERON

"**W**OULD YOU BOYS like to plant gardens?" my father said.

"Yes," we said.

"Good!" said my father. "I'll order a catalogue."

So it was settled. But afterward, Huey said to me, "What's a catalogue?"

"A catalogue," I said, "is where cats come from. It's a big book full of pictures of hundreds and hundreds of cats. And when you open it up, all the cats jump out and start running around."

"I don't believe you," Huey said.

"It's true," I said.

"But why would Dad be sending for that catalogue cat book?"

"The cats help with the garden," I said.

"I don't believe you," Huey said.

"It's true," I said. "You open the catalogue, and the cats jump out. Then they run outside and work in the garden. White cats dig up the ground with their claws. Black cats brush the ground smooth with their tails. Yellow and brown cats roll on the seeds and push them underground so they can grow."

"I don't believe you," Huey said. "Cats don't act like that."

"Of course," I said, "*ordinary* cats don't act like that. That's why you have to get them specially – catalogue cats."

"Really?" Huey said.

"Really," I said.

"I'm going to ask Dad about it," Huey said.

"You ask Dad about everything," I said. "Don't you think it's time you learned something on your own for a change?"

Huey looked hurt. "I do learn things by myself,' he said. "I wonder when the catalogue will come."

"Soon," I said.

The next morning Huey woke me up. "I dreamed about the catalogue cats!" he said. "Only in my dream the yellow and brown ones were washing the windows and painting the house! You don't suppose they could do that, do you?"

"No, they can't do that, Huey," I said. "They don't have a way to hold rags and paintbrushes."

"I suppose not," Huey said.

Every day Huey asked my father if the catalogue had come.

"Not yet," my father kept saying. He was very pleased that Huey was so interested in the garden.

Huey dreamed about the catalogue cats again. A whole team of them was carrying a giant squash to the house. One had his teeth around the stem. The others were pushing it with their shoulders and their heads.

"Do you think that's what they really do, Julian?" Huey said.

"Yes, they do that," I said.

Two weeks went by.

"Well, Huey and Julian," my father said, "today is the big day. The catalogue is here."

"The catalogue is here! The catalogue is here! The catalogue is here!" Huey said. He was dancing and twirling around.

I was thinking about going someplace else.

"What's the matter, Julian?" my father said. "Don't you want to see the catalogue?"

"Oh, yes, I – want to see it," I said.

My father had the catalogue under his arm. The three of us sat down on the couch.

"Open it!" Huey said.

My father opened the catalogue.

Inside were bright pictures of flowers and vegetables. The catalogue company would send you the seeds, and you could grow the flowers and vegetables.

Huey started turning the pages faster and faster. "Where are the cats? Where are the cats?" he kept saying.

"What cats?" my father said.

Huey started to cry.

My father looked at me. "Julian," he said, "please tell me what is going on."

"Huey thought catalogues were books with cats in them. Catalogue cats," I said.

Huey sobbed. "Julian told me! Special cats – cats that work in gardens! White ones – they dig up the dirt. Black ones – they brush the ground with their tails. Yellow and brown ones – they roll on the seeds." Huey was crying harder than ever.

"Julian!" said my father.

"Yes," I said. When my father's voice gets loud, mine gets so small I can only whisper.

"Julian," my father said, "didn't you tell Huey that the catalogue cats are invisible?"

"No," I said.

"Julian told me they jumped out of catalogues! He said they jumped out and work in gardens. As soon as you get the catalogue, they go to work."

"Well," said my father, "that's very ignorant. Julian has

127

never had a garden before in his life. I wouldn't trust a person who has never had a garden in his life to tell me about catalogue cats. Would you?"

"No," Huey said slowly. He was still crying a little.

My father pulled out his handkerchief and gave it to Huey. "Now, blow your nose and listen to me," my father said.

Huey blew his nose and sat up straight on the couch. I sat back and tried to be as small as I could.

"First of all," said my father, "a lot of people have wasted a lot of time trying to see catalogue cats. It's a waste of time because catalogue cats are the fastest animals alive. No one is as quick as a catalogue cat. It may be that they really *are* visible and that they just move so quickly you can't see them. But you can feel them. When you look for a catalogue cat over your right shoulder, you can feel that he is climbing the tree above your left ear. When you turn fast and look at the tree, you can feel that he has jumped out and landed behind your back. And then sometimes you feel all the little hairs on your backbone quiver – that's when you know a catalogue cat is laughing at you and telling you that you're wasting your time.

"Catalogue cats love gardens, and they love to work in gardens. However, they will only do half the work. If they are in the garden where people don't do any work, the catalogue cats will not do any work either. But if they are in a garden where people work hard, all the work will go twice as fast because of the catalogue cats."

"When you were a boy and had a garden," Huey said, "did your garden have catalogue cats?"

"Yes," my father said, "my garden had catalogue cats."

"And were they your friends?" Huey said.

"Well," my father said, "they like people, but they move too fast to make friends.

"That's one more thing," my father said. "Catalogue cats aren't *in* the garden catalogues, and no one can order catalogue cats. Catalogue cats are only *around* the companies the catalogues come from. You don't order them, you request them."

"I can write up a request," I said.

"Huey can do that very well, I'm sure," my father said, "if he would like to. Would you like to, Huey?"

Huey said he would.

My father got a piece of paper and pencil.

And Huey wrote it all down:

REQUESTED:
1 dozen catalogue cats,
all varieties,
WHOEVER
wants to come
is WELCOME.

STRAY

CYNTHIA RYLANT

IN JANUARY, A PUPPY wandered onto the property of Mr Amos Lacey and his wife, Mamie, and their daughter, Doris. Icicles hung three feet or more from the eaves of houses, snow-drifts swallowed up automobiles and the birds were so fluffed up they looked comic.

The puppy had been abandoned, and it made its way down the road towards the Laceys' small house, its ears tucked, its tail between its legs, shivering.

Doris, whose school had been called off because of the snow, was out shovelling the cinderblock front steps when she spotted the pup on the road. She set down the shovel.

"Hey! Come on!" she called.

The puppy stopped in the road, wagging its tail timidly, trembling with shyness and cold.

Doris trudged through the yard, went up the shovelled drive and met the dog.

"Come on, Pooch."

"Where did *that* come from?" Mrs Lacey asked as soon as Doris put the dog down in the kitchen.

Mr Lacey was at the table, cleaning his fingernails with his pocket-knife. The snow was keeping him home from his job at the warehouse.

"I don't know where it came from," he said mildly, "but I know for sure where it's going."

Doris hugged the puppy hard against her. She said nothing.

Because the roads would be too bad for travel for many days, Mr Lacey couldn't get out to take the puppy to the pound in the city right away. He agreed to let it sleep in the basement while Mrs Lacey grudgingly let Doris feed it table scraps. The woman was sensitive about throwing out food.

By the looks of it, Doris figured the puppy was about six months old, and on its way to being a big dog. She thought it might have some shepherd in it.

Four days passed and the puppy did not complain. It never cried in the night or howled at the wind. It didn't tear up everything in the basement. It wouldn't even follow Doris up the basement steps unless it was invited.

It was a good dog.

Several times Doris had opened the door in the kitchen that led to the basement and the puppy had been there, all stretched out, on the top step. Doris knew it had wanted some company and that it had lain against the door, listening to the talk in the kitchen, smelling the food, being a part of things. It always wagged its tail, eyes all sleepy, when she found it there.

Even after a week had gone by, Doris didn't name the dog. She knew her parents wouldn't let her keep it, that her father made so little money any pets were out of the question, and that the pup would definitely go to the pound when the weather cleared.

Still, she tried talking to them about the dog at dinner one night.

"She's a good dog, isn't she?" Doris said, hoping one of them would agree with her.

Her parents glanced at each other and went on eating.

"She's not much trouble," Doris added. "I like her." She smiled at them, but they continued to ignore her.

"I figure she's real smart," Doris said to her mother. "I could teach her things."

Mrs Lacey just shook her head and stuffed a forkful of sweet potato in her mouth. Doris fell silent, praying the weather would never clear.

But on Saturday, nine days after the dog had arrived, the sun was shining and the roads were ploughed. Mr Lacey opened up the trunk of his car and came into the house.

Doris was sitting alone in the living room, hugging a pillow and rocking back and forth on the edge of a chair. She was trying not to cry but she was not strong enough. Her face was wet and red, her eyes full of distress.

Mrs Lacey looked into the room from the doorway.

"Mama," Doris said in a small voice. "Please."

Mrs Lacey shook her head.

"You know we can't afford a dog, Doris. You try to act more grown-up about this."

Doris pressed her face into the pillow.

Outside, she heard the trunk of the car slam shut, one of the doors open and close, the old engine cough and choke and finally start up.

"Daddy," she whispered. "Please."

She heard the car travel down the road, and, though it was early afternoon, she could do nothing but go to her bed. She cried herself to sleep, and her dreams were full of searching and searching for things lost.

It was nearly night when she finally woke up. Lying there, like stone, still exhausted, she wondered if she would ever in her life have anything. She stared at the wall for a while.

But she started feeling hungry, and she knew she'd have to make herself get out of bed and eat some dinner. She wanted not to go into the kitchen, past the basement door. She wanted not to face her parents.

But she rose up heavily.

Her parents were sitting at the table, dinner over, drinking coffee. They looked at her when she came in, but she kept her head down. No one spoke.

Doris made herself a glass of powdered milk and drank it all down. Then she picked up a cold biscuit and started out of the room.

"You'd better feed that mutt before it dies of starvation," Mr Lacey said.

Doris turned around.

"What?"

"I said, you'd better feed your dog. I figure it's looking for you."

Doris put her hand to her mouth.

"You didn't take her?" she asked.

"Oh, I took her all right," her father answered. "Worst looking place I've ever seen. Ten dogs to a cage. Smell was enough to knock you down. And they give an animal six

133

days to live. Then they kill it with some kind of a shot."

Doris stared at her father.

"I wouldn't leave an *ant* in that place," he said. "So I brought the dog back."

Mrs Lacey was smiling at him and shaking her head as if she would never, ever, understand him.

Mr Lacey sipped his coffee.

"Well," he said, "are you going to feed it or not?"

THE STOLEN BICYCLE

WILLIAM SAROYAN

THIS MOVIE OF 1919 was full of high spirits, recklessness, and excellent timing, so that when Ike George left the theatre he himself was like a man in a movie: full of energy, afraid of nothing, and eager to get on with his life.

As if it were not himself, as if it were not wrong to do so, he took the brand-new bike out of the bicycle rack in front of the theatre, and, in full view of the whole world, rode away on it.

Johnny Faragoh, who sold bicycles for Kebo the Jap, was standing in front of his house on L Street.

As the boy rode by, Johnny noticed the new bike.

"Hey, kid!" he called out.

The boy turned in the street and coasted up. He knew Johnny. If he called you, you had to stop. It was a pleasure for the boy, though: he had always admired Johnny, who was like somebody in a movie himself.

"That's a swell bike," Johnny said. "Where'd you get it?"

"Mr York gave it to me for my birthday," the boy said.

135

"You mean the guy who's in charge of street sales for *The Herald*?"

"Yeah."

The boy got off the bike and let the older one take the handlebars. Johnny lifted the bike, bounced it, sat on it, and very easily began riding around in a small circle.

"He gave you a good one, boy. What's your name?"

"Ike."

"Ike what?"

"Ike George," the boy said.

"You anything to *Cookie* George?"

"He's my cousin."

"First or second?"

"First."

"Cookie's a good friend of mine," Johnny said.

"He's always in trouble," Ike said.

"Where'd you steal it?" Johnny said. "You can tell *me*."

"I didn't steal it," Ike said. "Mr York gave it to me for my birthday."

"Cookie's my pal," Johnny said. "Somebody else gave it to you. That guy York wouldn't give you a bike if you saved his life."

"He gave me *this* bike," the boy said.

"Tell them Cookie gave it to you," Johnny said. "Somebody'll go and ask York and you'll get in trouble."

"Cookie's got no money," the boy said.

"Sometimes he has and sometimes he hasn't," Johnny said. "I'm going to see him tonight," Johnny said. "I'll tell him about it. Go on home now."

The boy got on the bicycle and rode home.

When his father saw the bicycle he said, "Haig, where did you get that bicycle?"

"Cookie gave it to me," the boy said.

"You mean your cousin Gourken?"

"Yes," the boy said.

"Gourken has no money," the boy's father said. "You've borrowed it, haven't you?"

"No," the boy said. "It's mine."

"Go inside and eat your supper," the father said.

The boy went inside and ate his supper. It took him less than five minutes. When he came out of the house his father was riding the bike in the yard.

"Haig," the father said, "take the bicycle back where you got it. You're no thief."

"Cookie gave it to me," the boy said.

The next day he rode the bicycle to school, just the way it was. He didn't turn it over and hammer out the numbers the way you were supposed to do. The numbers were 137620R. After school he rode the bicycle to *The Evening Herald*, and told everybody his cousin Cookie had given it to him for a birthday present.

"What's your birthday?" his friend Nick Roma asked him.

"September 7, 1909," the boy said.

"This is May," Nick said. "You'll get in trouble, Ike."

He rode the bicycle to his corner, Mariposa and Eye, and sold papers all afternoon. Cookie came to the corner in the evening. "Is this the bike?" he said.

"Yeah," the boy said.

"I sure gave you a good one, didn't I?"

"Yeah. Thanks."

By October he had almost forgotten how the bicycle had come into his possession. In November the chain broke while he was sprinting. The rim of the front wheel broke and the fork buckled. It cost him a dollar-and-a-quarter for a new rim. Another dollar to have the buckled fork replaced by a straight second-hand one, and fifty cents for labour.

After that the bike was his, out and out.

One day, a year after he had taken the bike from the rack in front of the Liberty Theatre, he put it back into the rack, and went on in and saw the show.

When he came out, the bike was gone. He walked home, and when he saw his father he said, "They stole my bike."

"That's all right," his father said. "Go inside and eat your supper."

"I'm not hungry," the boy said. "If I catch the fellow who stole it, I'll give him the worst beating he ever got."

"Go inside and eat," the boy's father said.

"I don't want to eat," the boy said.

He stood before his father, very angry, and then suddenly turned and ran. He ran all the way to town and walked along every street looking for his bike. After an hour he walked home, ate his supper, and went to bed.

He was now eleven years old.

One evening in August he was playing handball with Nick Roma against the wall of the Telephone Building. Nick made a man-killer, a truck turned into the alley, bumped the ball, and carried it down the alley. The boy went after the ball. It had fallen down a small flight of stairs into a narrow passageway where there were dustbins and boxes full of ashes. He looked for the ball. In a corner he saw a bicycle frame, with the paint scratched off. He turned the frame upside down and read the number. It had been hammered, but he could still read the 13 and the R.

He stood in the dark passageway, holding the old frame. His friend Nick Roma came up and said, "Where's the ball?"

"It's lost," the boy said. "I found my bike. They took everything off of it,"

"Is the frame all right?" Nick said.

"It's all right," the boy said, "but what good is a frame without the other stuff?"

"It's worth *something*," Nick said.

"I'd like to get the guy who stole it," the boy said.

Paul Armer came walking down the alley and saw the two boys with the bicycle frame.

He examined the frame with them.

"What do you want for it, Ike?" he said.

"I don't know," the boy said.

He was angry and broken-hearted.

"It was my bike," he said to Paul. "Then they stole it. We were playing handball, I went to get the ball and I found the frame. They took everything off of it and threw it in here."

"Where did the ball go?" Nick said.

"To hell with the ball," Ike said.

"I'll give you a dollar for it," Paul Armer said.

"All right," the boy said.

A week later when he saw the bike again, painted and with new parts, he became angry again and said to himself, "If I ever get the guy who stole it!"

THE GENERAL SEES ACTIVE
SERVICE

ETHEL TURNER

from Seven Little Australians

*The seven little Australians are the children of Captain Woolcot of
Sydney. His first wife has died and his young second wife, Esther, is
the mother of "the General", the baby of the family. After a rebellion
by the children against bread-and-butter nursery tea, the Captain has
cancelled the children's visit to the pantomime in punishment . . .*

IT WAS A DAY AFTER "the events narrated in the last
chapter," as story-book parlance has it. And Judy, with
a wrathful look in her eyes, was sitting on the nursery
table, her knees touching her chin and her thin brown
hands clasped round them.

"It's a shame," she said, "it's a burning, wicked shame!
What's the use of fathers in the world, I'd like to know!"

"Oh, Judy!" said Meg, who was curled up in an
armchair, deep in a book. But she said it mechanically, and
only as a matter of duty, being three years older than Judy.

"Think of the times we could have if he didn't live with
us," Judy continued, calmly disregardful.

"Why, we'd have fowl three times a day, and the pantomime seven nights a week."

Nell suggested that it was not quite usual to have pantomimic performances on the seventh day, but Judy was not daunted.

"I'd have a kind of church pantomime," she said thoughtfully – " beautiful pictures and things about the Holy Land, and the loveliest music, and beautiful children in white, singing hymns, and bright colours all about, and no collection plates to take your only threepenny bit – oh! and no sermons or litanies, of course."

"Oh, Judy!" murmured Meg, turning a leaf.

Judy unclasped her hands, and then clasped them again more tightly than before. "Six whole tickets wasted – thirty beautiful shillings – just because we have a father!"

"He sent them to the Digby-Smiths," Bunty volunteered, "and wrote on the envelope, *"With compts. –* J.C. Woolcot.'"

Judy moaned. "Six horrid little Digby-Smiths sitting in the theatre watching our fun with their six horrid little eyes," she said bitterly.

Bunty, who was mathematically inclined, wanted to know why they wouldn't look at it through their twelve horrid little eyes, and Judy laughed and came down from the table, after expressing a wicked wish that the little Digby-Smiths might all tumble over the dress-circle rail before the curtain rose. Meg shut her book with a hurried bang.

"Has Pip gone yet? Father'll be awfully cross. Oh *dear*, what a head I've got!" she said. "Where's Esther? Has anyone seen Esther?"

"My *dear* Meg!" Judy said; "why, it's at least two hours since Esther went up the drive before your very nose. She's gone to Waverly – why, she came in and told you, and said she trusted you to see about the coat, and you said, "M – 'm! all right."

Meg gave a startled look of recollection. "Did I have to

141

clean it?" she asked in a frightened tone, and pushing her fair hair back from her forehead.

"Oh, girls! what *was* it I had to do?"

"Clean with benzine, iron while wet, put in a cool place to keep warm, and bake till brown," said Judy promptly. "Surely you heard, Margaret? Esther was at such pains to explain."

Meg ruffled her hair again despairingly. "What shall I do?" she said, actual tears springing to her eyes. "What will Father say? Oh, Judy, you might have reminded me."

Nell slipped an arm round her neck. "She's only teasing, Megsie; Esther did it and left it ready in the hall – you've only to give it to Pip. Pat has to take the dogcart into town this afternoon to have the back seat mended, and Pip's going in it, too, that's all, and they're putting the horse in now; you're not late."

It was the coat Bunty had done his best to spoil that all the trouble was about. It belonged, as I said, to the Captain's full-dress uniform, and was wanted for a dinner at the Barracks this same evening. And Esther had been sponging and cleaning at it all the morning, and had left directions that it was to be taken to the Barracks in the afternoon.

Presently the dogcart came spinning round to the door in great style, Pip driving and Pat looking sulkily on. They took the coat parcel and put it carefully under the seat, and were preparing to start again, when Judy came out upon the veranda, holding the General in an uncomfortable position in her arms.

"You come, too, Fizz, there's heaps of room – there's no reason you shouldn't," Pip said suddenly.

"Oh – h – h!" said Judy, her eyes sparkling. She took a rapid step forward and lifted her foot to get in.

"Oh, I say!" remonstrated Pip, "you'll have to put on something over that dress, old girl – it's all over jam and things,"

Judy shot herself into the hall and returned with her

142

ulster; she set the General on the floor for a minute while she donned it, then picked him up and handed him up to Pip.

"He'll have to come, too," she said; "I promised Esther I wouldn't let him out of my sight for a minute; she's getting quite nervous about him lately – thinks he'll get broken."

Pip grumbled a minute or two, but the General gave a gurgling, captivating laugh and held up his arms, so he took him up and held him while Judy clambered in.

"We can come back in the tram to the Quay, and then get a boat back," she said, squeezing the baby on the seat between them. "The General loves going on the water."

Away they sped; down the neglected carriage drive, out of the gates, and away down the road. Pip, Judy of the shining eyes, the General devouring his thumb, and Pat smiling-faced once more because in possession of the reins.

A wind from the river swept through the belt of gum trees on the Crown lands, and sent the young red blood leaping through their veins; it played havoc with Judy's curls, and dyed her brown cheeks a warm red; it made the General kick and laugh and grow restive, and caused Pip to stick his hat on the back of his head and whistle joyously.

Until town was reached, when they were forced to yield somewhat to the claims of conventionality.

On the way to Paddington a gentleman on horseback slackened pace a little. Pip took off his hat with a flourish, and Judy gave a frank, pleased smile, for it was a certain old Colonel they had known for years, and had cause to remember his good-humour and liberality.

"Well, my little maid – well, Philip, lad," he said, smiling genially, while his horse danced round the dogcart – " and the General too – where are you all off to?"

"The Barracks – I'm taking something up for the governor," Pip answered. Judy was watching the plunging horse with admiring eyes. "And then we're going back home."

The old gentleman managed, in spite of the horse's tricks, to slip his hand in his pocket. "Here's something to make yourselves ill with on the way," he said, handing them two half-crowns; "but don't send me the doctor's bill."

He flicked the General's cheek with his whip, gave Judy a nod, and cantered off.

The children looked at each other with sparkling eyes.

"Coconuts," Pip said, "and tarts and toffee, and save the rest for a football?" Judy shook her head.

"Where do *I* come in?" she said. "You'd keep the football at school. I vote pink jujubes, and ice-creams, and a wax doll."

"A wax grandmother!" Pip retorted; "you wouldn't be such a girl, I hope." Then he added, with almost pious fervour, "Thank goodness you've always hated dolls, Fizz."

Judy gave a sudden leap in her seat, almost upsetting the General, and bringing down upon her head a storm of reproaches from the coachman. "*I* know!" she said; "and we're almost half-way there now. Oh – h – h! it "*will* be lovely."

Pip urged her to explain herself.

"Bondi Aquarium – skating, boats, merry-go-round, switchback threepence a go!" she returned succinctly.

"Good iron," Pip whistled softly, while he revolved the thing in his mind. "There'd be something over, too, to get some tucker with, and perhaps something for the football, too." Then his brow clouded.

"There's the kid – whatever did you go bringing him for? Just like a girl, to spoil everything!"

Judy looked nonplussed. "I quite forgot him," she said, vexedly. "Couldn't we leave him somewhere? Couldn't we ask someone to take care of him while we go? Oh, it would be *too* bad to have to give it up just because of him. It's beginning to rain, too; we couldn't take him with us."

They were at the foot of Barrack Hill now, and Pat told them they must get out and walk the rest of the way up, or he would never get the dogcart finished to take back that evening.

Pip tumbled out and took the General, all in a bunched-up heap, and Judy alighted carefully after him, the precious coat parcel in her arms. And they walked up the asphalt hill to the gate leading to the officers' quarters in utter silence.

"Well?" Pip said querulously, as they reached the top. "Be quick; haven't you thought of anything?"

That levelling of brows, and pursing of lips, always meant deep and intricate calculation on his sister's part, as he knew full well.

"Yes," Judy said quietly. "I've got a plan that will do, I think." Then a sudden fire entered her manner.

"Who is the General's father? Tell me that," she said in a rapid, eager way; "and isn't it right and proper fathers should look after their sons? And doesn't he deserve we should get even with him for doing us out of the pantomime? And isn't the Aquarium too lovely to miss?"

"Well?" Pip said; his slower brain did not follow such rapid reasoning.

"Only I'm going to leave the General here at the Barracks for a couple of hours till we come back, his father being the proper person to watch over him." Judy grasped the General's small fat hand in a determined way, and opened the gate.

"Oh, I say," remarked Pip, "we'll get in an awful row, you know, Fizz. I don't think we'd better – I don't really, old girl."

"Not a bit," said Judy stoutly – "at least, only a bit, and the Aquarium's worth that. Look how it's raining; the child will get croup, or rheumatism, or something if we take him; there's Father standing over on the green near the tennis-court talking to a man. I'll slip quietly along the veranda and into his own room, and put the coat and the General on the bed; then I'll tell a soldier to go and tell Father his parcels have come, and while he's gone I'll fly back to you, and we'll catch the tram and go to the Aquarium."

Pip whistled again, softly. He was used to bold proposals from this sister of his, but this was beyond everything. "B – b – but," he said uneasily, "but, Judy, whatever would he do with that kid for two mortal hours?"

"Mind him," Judy returned promptly. "It's a pretty thing if a father can't mind his own child for two hours. Afterwards, you see, when we've been to the Aquarium, we will come back and fetch him, and we can explain to Father how it was raining, and that we thought we'd better not take him with us for fear of rheumatism, and that we were in a hurry to catch the tram, and as he wasn't in his room we just put him on the bed till he came. Why, Pip, it's beautifully simple!"

Pip still looked uncomfortable. "I don't like it, Fizz," he said again; "he'll be in a fearful wax."

Judy gave him one exasperated look. "Go and see if that's the Bondi tram coming," she said; and, glad of a moment's respite, he went down the path again to the pavement and looked down the hill. When he turned round again she had gone.

He stuck his hands in his pockets and walked up and down the path a few times. "Fizz'll get us hanged yet," he muttered, looking darkly at the door in the wall through which she had disappeared.

He pushed his hat to the back of his head and stared gloomily at his boots, wondering what would be the consequences of this new mischief. There was a light footfall beside him.

"Come on," said Judy, pulling his sleeve; "It's done now, come on, let's go and have our fun; have you got the money safe?"

It was two o'clock as they passed out of the gate and turned their faces up the hill to the tram stopping-place. And it was half-past four when they jumped out of a town-bound tram and entered the gates again to pick up their charge.

Such an afternoon as they had had! Once inside the Aquarium, even Pip had put his conscience qualms on one side, and bent all his energies to enjoying himself thoroughly. And Judy was like a little mad thing. She spent a shilling of her money on the switchback railway, pronouncing the swift, bewildering motion "heavenly." The first journey made Pip feel sick, so he eschewed a repetition of it, and watched Judy go off from time to time,

waving gaily from the perilous little car, almost with his heart in his mouth. Then they hired a pair of roller skates each, and bruised themselves black and blue with heavy falls on the asphalt. After that they had a ride on the merry-go-round, but Judy found it tame after the switchback, and refused to squander a second threepence upon it, contenting herself with watching Pip fly round, and madly running by his side to keep up as long as she could. They finished the afternoon with a prolonged inspection of the fish-tanks, a light repast of jam tarts of questionable freshness, and twopennyworth of peanuts. And, as I said, it was half-past four as they hastened up the path again to the top gate of the Barracks.

"I *hope* he's been good," Judy said, as she turned the handle. "Yes, you come, too, Pip" – for that young gentleman hung back one agonised second. "Twenty kicks or blows divided by two only make ten, you see."

They went up the long stone veranda and stopped at one door.

There was a little knot of young officers laughing and talking close by.

"Take my word, 'twas as good as a play to see Wooly grabbing his youngster, and stuffing it into a cab, and getting in himself, all with a look of ponderous injured dignity," one said, and laughed at the recollection.

Another blew away a cloud of cigar smoke. "It was a jolly little beggar," he said. "It doubled its fists and landed His High Mightiness one in the eye; and then its shoe dropped off, and we all rushed to pick it up, and it was muddy and generally dilapidated, and old Wooly went red slowly up to his ear-tips as he tried to put it on."

A little figure stepped into the middle of the group – a little figure with an impossibly short and shabby ulster, thin black-stockinged legs, and a big hat crushed over a tangle of curls.

"It is my father you are speaking of," she said, her head very high, her tone haughty, "and I cannot tell where your

149

amusement is. Is my father here, or did I hear you say he had gone away?"

Two of the men looked foolish, the third took off his cap.

"I am sorry you should have overheard us, Miss Woolcot," he said pleasantly. "Still, there is no irreparable harm done, is there? Yes, your father has gone away in a cab. He couldn't imagine how the little boy came on his bed, and, as he couldn't keep him here very well, I suppose he has taken him home."

Something like a look of shame came into Judy's bright eyes.

"I am afraid I must have put my father to some inconvenience," she said quietly. "It was I who left the Gen – my brother here, because I didn't know what to do with him for an hour or two. But I quite meant to take him home myself. Has he been gone long?"

"About half an hour," the officer said, and tried not to look amused at the little girl's old-fashioned manner.

"Ah, thank you. Perhaps we can catch him up. Come on, Pip," and, nodding in a grave, distant manner, she turned away, and went down the veranda and through the gate with her brother.

"A nice hole we're in," he said.

Judy nodded.

"It's about the very awfullest thing we've ever done in our lives. Fancy the governor carting that child all the way from here! Oh, lor'!"

Judy nodded again.

"Can't you speak?" he said irritably. "You've got us into this – I didn't want to do it; but I'll stand by you, of course. Only you'll have to think of something quick."

Judy bit three finger-tips off her right-hand glove, and looked melancholy.

"There's absolutely nothing to do, Pip," she said slowly. "I didn't think it would turn out like this. I suppose we'd better just go straight back and hand ourselves over for punishment. He'll be too angry to hear any sort of an

excuse, so we'd better just grin and bear whatever he does
to us. I'm really sorry, too, that I made a laughing-stock of
him up there."

Pip was explosive. He called her a little ass and a gowk
and a stupid idiot for doing such a thing, and she did not
reproach him or answer back once.

They caught a tram and went into Sydney, and
afterwards to the boat. They ensconced themselves in a
corner at the far end, and discussed the state of affairs with
much seriousness. Then Pip got up and strolled about a
little to relieve his feelings, coming back in a second with a
white, scared face.

"He's on the boat," he said, in a horrified whisper.

"Where – where – where? What – what – what?" Judy
cried, unintentionally mimicking a long-buried monarch.

"In the cabin, looking as glum as a boiled wallaby, and
hanging on to the poor little General as if he thinks he'll fly
away."

Judy looked a little frightened for the first time.

"Can't we hide? Don't let him see us. It wouldn't be any

good offering to take the General now. We're in for it now; Pip – there'll be no quarter."

Pip groaned; then Judy stood up.

"Let's creep down as far as the engine," she said, "and see if he does look very bad."

They made their way cautiously along the deck, and took up a position where they could see without being seen. The dear little General was sitting on the seat next to his stern father, who had a firm hold of the back of his woolly pelisse. He was sucking his little dirty hand, and casting occasional longing glances at his tan shoe, which he knew was delicious to bite. Once or twice he had pulled it off and conveyed it to his mouth, but his father intercepted it, and angrily buttoned it on again in its rightful place. He wanted, too, to slither off the horrid seat, and crawl all over the deck, and explore the ground under the seats, and see where the puffing noise came from; but there was that iron grasp on his coat that no amount of wriggling would move. No wonder the poor child looked unhappy!

At last the boat stopped at a wharf not far from Misrule, and the Captain alighted, carrying his small dirty son gingerly in his arms. He walked slowly up the red road along which the dogcart had sped so blithesomely some six or seven hours ago, and Judy and Pip followed at a respectful – a very respectful – distance. At the gate he saw them, and gave a large, angry beckon for them to come up. Judy went very white, but obeyed instantly, and Pip, pulling himself together, brought up the rear.

Afterwards Judy only had a very indistinct remembrance of what happened during the next half-hour. She knew there was a stormy scene, in which Esther and the whole family came in for an immense amount of vituperation.

Then Pip received a thrashing, in spite of Judy's persistent avowal that it was all her fault, and Pip hadn't done anything. She remembered wondering whether she would be treated as summarily as Pip, so angry was her father's face as he pushed the boy aside and stood looking at her, riding whip in hand.

But he flung it down and laid a heavy hand on her shrinking shoulder.

"Next Monday," he said slowly – "next Monday morning you will go to boarding school. Esther, kindly see Helen's clothes are ready for boarding school – next Monday morning."

I SPY

GRAHAM GREENE

CHARLIE STOWE WAITED until he heard his mother snore before he got out of bed. Even then he moved with caution and tiptoed to the window. The front of the house was irregular, so that it was possible to see a light burning in his mother's room. But now all the windows were dark. A searchlight passed across the sky, lighting the banks of cloud and probing the dark deep spaces between, seeking enemy airships. The wind blew from the sea, and Charlie Stowe could hear behind his mother's snores the beating of the waves. A draught through the cracks in the window-frame stirred his night-shirt. Charlie Stowe was frightened.

But the thought of the tobacconist's shop which his father kept down a dozen wooden stairs drew him on. He was twelve years old, and already boys at the County School mocked him because he had never smoked a cigarette. The packets were piled twelve deep below, Gold Flake and Player's, De Reszke, Abdulla, Woodbines, and the little shop lay under a thin haze of stale smoke which would completely disguise his crime. That it was a crime to steal some of his father's stock Charlie Stowe had no doubt, but he did not love his father; his father was unreal to him, a wraith, pale, thin, indefinite, who noticed him only spasmodically and left even punishment to his mother. For his mother he felt a passionate demonstrative love; her large boisterous presence and her noisy charity filled the world for him; from her speech he judged her the friend of everyone, from the rector's wife to the "dear Queen", except the "Huns", the monsters who lurked in Zeppelins in the clouds. But his father's affection and dislike were as indefinite as his movements. Tonight he had said he would be in Norwich, and yet you never knew. Charlie Stowe had no sense of safety as he crept down the wooden stairs. When they creaked he clenched his fingers on the collar of his night-shirt.

At the bottom of the stairs he came out quite suddenly into the little shop. It was too dark to see his way, and he did not dare touch the switch. For half a minute he sat in despair on the bottom step with his chin cupped in his hands. Then the regular movement of the searchlight was reflected through an upper window and the boy had time to fix in memory the pile of cigarettes, the counter, and the small hole under it. The footsteps of a policeman on the pavement made him grab the first packet to his hand and dive for the hole. A light shone along the floor and a hand tried the door, then the footsteps passed on, and Charlie cowered in the darkness.

At last he got his courage back by telling himself in his curiously adult way that if he were caught now there was nothing to be done about it, and he might as well have his smoke. He put a cigarette in his mouth and then remembered that he had no matches. For a while he dared not move. Three times the searchlight lit the shop, as he muttered taunts and encouragements. "May as well be hung for a sheep," "Cowardy, cowardy custard," grown-up and childish exhortations oddly mixed.

But as he moved he heard footfalls in the street, the sound of several men walking rapidly. Charlie Stowe was old enough to feel surprise that anybody was about. The footsteps came nearer, stopped; a key was turned in the shop door, a voice said: "Let him in," and then he heard his father, "If you wouldn't mind being quiet, gentlemen. I don't want to wake up the family." There was a note unfamiliar to Charlie in the undecided voice. A torch flashed and the electric globe burst into blue light. The boy held his breath; he wondered whether his father would hear his heart beating, and he clutched his night-shirt tightly and prayed, "O God, don't let me be caught." Through a crack in the counter he could see his father where he stood, one hand held to his high stiff collar, between two men in bowler hats and belted mackintoshes. They were strangers.

"Have a cigarette," his father said in a voice dry as a biscuit. One of the men shook his head. "It wouldn't do, not when we are on duty. Thank you all the same." He spoke gently, but without kindness: Charlie Stowe thought his father must be ill.

"Mind if I put a few in my pocket?" Mr Stowe asked, and when the man nodded he lifted a pile of Gold Flake and Player's from a shelf and caressed the packets with the tips of his fingers.

"Well," he said, "there's nothing to be done about it, and I may as well have my smokes." For a moment Charlie Stowe feared discovery, his father stared round the shop so thoroughly; he might have been seeing it for the first time. "It's a good little business," he said, "for those that like it. The wife will sell out, I suppose. Else the neighbours'll be wrecking it. Well, you want to be off. A stitch in time. I'll get my coat."

"One of us'll come with you, if you don't mind," said the stranger gently.

"You needn't trouble. It's on the peg here. There, I'm all ready."

The other man said in an embarrassed way, "Don't you want to speak to your wife?" The thin voice was decided, "Not me. Never do today what you can put off till tomorrow. She'll have her chance later, won't she?"

"Yes, yes," one of the strangers said and he became very cheerful and encouraging. "Don't you worry too much. While there's life . . . " and suddenly his father tried to laugh.

When the door had closed Charlie Stowe tiptoed upstairs and got into bed. He wondered why his father had left the house again so late at night and who the strangers were. Surprise and awe kept him for a little while awake. It was as if a familiar photograph had stepped from the frame to reproach him with neglect. He remembered how his father had held tight to his collar and fortified himself with proverbs, and he thought for the first time that, while his mother was boisterous and kindly, his father was very like himself, doing things in the dark which frightened him. It would have pleased him to go down to his father and tell him that he loved him, but he could hear through the window the quick steps going away. He was alone in the house with his mother, and he fell asleep.

A TERRIBLE ANNOUNCEMENT

LYNNE REID BANKS

from One More River

I**T WOULDN'T HAVE BEEN** so bad if Lesley had had any warning. Or rather, if she'd heeded the warning signs.

She had to admit, long afterwards, that there had been some. She'd just ignored them. Life was so exciting and full at the time that any shadow that fell on her, any suspicion of a shadow even, she simply darted out from under and danced blithely on her way as if it weren't there. She wasn't prepared to admit that anything could go wrong, that anything could ever change.

The shadow, such as it was, was in her parents' manner.

Lesley loved both her parents, though some doubts occasionally crossed her mind about her father. He was always lovely to *her*, and to her mother; in addition, he was handsome, successful, and generous. But Lesley could never quite forget that awful business about her brother, Noah – she'd never understood about that.

Noah was much older than she was – eight years – but a brother was a brother. To exile him from the family, to never speak about him, because of religion . . . Well, of course they were an Orthodox family, they kept kosher and went to synagogue and so on, and she knew her parents felt very strongly Jewish. Still, it didn't fully make sense to Lesley, and it couldn't help seeming to her sometimes as if her father had behaved – not very well about it.

But that was a long time ago. Three years now . . . She'd been told to forget about it, and if she hadn't, quite, it was only because nobody had really explained it all to her, so it nagged at her mind like a locked door.

Aside from that, life was good, it was almost one hundred per cent perfect as a matter of fact, what with having rich parents, being nice-looking (most people said), well up on schoolwork, good at sports, and now having the most exciting boyfriend in the entire eighth grade. She was comfortably aware that she was envied, but that didn't really affect her popularity. What more could anyone want?

So the funny atmosphere at home – the little glances, the conversations that stopped as she came into a room, the talk she could just hear through her bedroom floor long after she'd gone to bed instead of the friendly sounds of television – none of these really impinged on her happiness and her confidence that life in general was great, and would go on being great forever.

One bright, crunchy September day, the sort of prairie fall day that always made her feel her very best, Lesley came home from school a little later than usual, having stopped off at her friend Sonia's for a bacon sandwich and a good old gossip.

All the talk was about the junior Thanksgiving dance in early October. Happily, they'd both been invited in good time. Sonia's partner was in ninth grade, a grade ahead of the girls, and this made her, for once, more envied than Lesley, but Lesley liked her enough not to mind.

Anyway, she had Lee. He was just too wonderful. Tall, handsome, a basketball star, hot stuff in the drama club –

159

everything. He was also Jewish, which meant no objections from her parents. He and she had swapped class rings to show they were going steady. And now all she could think about – apart from who was going with whom to the dance – was her trip to the store on Saturday with her mother, to pick out a really gorgeous dress for the occasion.

"I wonder if they've got a strapless one in *midnight blue* satin?" she'd said dreamily. "Lee likes me in blue, he says I've got blue lights in my hair."

"You're so lucky!" Sonia had said (she was always saying it). "Your dad *owning* Shelby's! I can't imagine just being able to walk into the Junior Miss department and pick out the shooshiest gown in the place and say, 'That one!' and not even have your mom look at the price tag."

"Yeah, it's nice," said Lesley. She didn't know she sounded smug. Her father owning the best store in town was part of what made life good, but she was also used to it. It had always been the same, from the time when it was the *toy* department she could pick things from.

Before she'd left Sonia's, she'd gone to the bathroom and gargled with some undiluted Listerine. Disgusting taste! – but she couldn't risk either of her parents smelling the bacon on her breath. Bacon wasn't kosher, especially not with a glass of milk! She washed the slight guilt away with the grease, said so long and see you tomorrow to Sonia, and walked home through the familiar streets with her school-bag over her shoulder, full of dreams of a long, low-cut blue satin dress that set off her hair and her newly developed figure.

Her father was home – his car was in the drive. She peered in through the front window with the ruched curtains into the big, elegant living room. Yes, there he was, and there was her mother, too, talking as usual. . . . She tapped on the window.

They both jumped and their heads snapped around. It flashed through Lesley's mind that if they'd knocked on Sonia's window while Lesley had been eating the bacon sandwich, she'd have jumped just like that. What were they up to?

The shadow came close suddenly. But she ducked out from under it and ran up the wide front steps. She didn't know the shadow was following her and that this time she couldn't escape it.

As she let herself in through the gleaming white front door, her father appeared in the double doors of the living room. He wasn't tall like Lee's father. He was short and stocky, but strong-looking, though recently he had put on some weight. He had a full head of grey, curly hair that Lesley loved to play with. He was always immaculately dressed and polished his shoes – very good ones – every single night. That used to be Noah's job, Lesley suddenly remembered, a second before it registered that her father was not smiling his invariable welcome-home smile.

"Come in here, Les, will you? We want to talk to you."

She dismissed the shadow. Talk to her? Why not? She bounced into the living room and parked herself on the wide, brocaded arm of the chair he'd been sitting in.

"Hi, Mom! Am I about to be let in on the secret?" she asked perkily.

Her mother jumped again – well, her eyes did. "Secret?"

"Sure! I knew you'd tell me when you were ready."

Her parents exchanged one of those funny looks, and she knew she'd hit it right. She felt rather pleased at having been smarter than they thought. But that feeling gave way almost at once to unease because neither of them looked as if the secret were a nice one.

Her father sat down in the chair beside her. She put her arm around his shoulders and started to play with his hair, but he said, "Les, will you sit over there, please, where I can see you?"

Chilled, she moved. Her father was looking at her very seriously. Her mother was smiling, but nervously – she put her finger into her mouth very daintily and bit on a hang-nail.

"Is it something I've done?" Lesley asked, the bacon sandwich lurking in her conscience.

"No, no," they both said at once. And her father said, "It's something we're all going to do."

"Something tremendously exciting!" said her mother brightly.

Ah! Now Lesley knew. It was about Christmas. At last they'd seen sense! Lee's family went skiing in the Rockies every year at a Jewish resort, and for them there were no problems about parties and a tree and carol-singing and all the stuff Jews weren't supposed to do but that, if you stayed home, it was impossible to keep the rules about. Lesley had been hinting for months. She jumped up and let out a yell of happiness.

"We're going to go skiing!" she cried, clapping her hands.

"We're going to emigrate," said her father.

There was a brief pause. The words dropped into Lesley's mind innocently, like any other words, and there exploded like a bomb. Every muscle in her face went slack. Her arms fell to her sides. Everything in the room shrank away for a second and then came rushing back as if to crush her.

Her eyes went to her mother. She would take it back – she must. Because emigrating meant leaving Canada. Permanently. And that couldn't be true. It couldn't be what her father had said, or meant.

But her mother was nodding. Nodding and smiling like a doll. *Yes* she was nodding, as if it were quite possible and reasonable, yes. But it must be no. No. No. It *must* be.

Lesley felt the shadow falling around her like a heavy canvas, but she fought it off.

"What do you mean?" she said without raising her voice, though she was almost screaming inside.

"Sit down, Lesley, and listen to what I'm going to tell you."

Something went flash in Lesley's head. This had happened before. It had happened three years ago when her father had told her that Noah was disgraced, that he had left their faith, and that he wasn't part of them any more. *Part of us . . . He's not part of us.* The words came back.

But what were *they* part of? What was her father tearing to bits now?

She found herself sitting in the big chair, clinging to its arms. Her eyes were fixed on her father and the shadow was all around her so that she could hardly see him.

"We're Jews," he said (and this, too, was like that other time). "And we're Canadians. It's becoming harder and harder to remember which comes first. My father knew, because he came from the Old Country. And your

164

grandmother" – he nodded towards Lesley's mother – "she was first-generation, too. She knew. They brought us up to know that the most important thing for a Jew is to survive *as a Jew*. To keep faith with the past."

Lesley began to pant. What was he talking about?

"But Mom keeps kosher," she gasped. "We go to *shul*. And you're forever telling me—"

"Jewishness isn't a matter of what you're told. It's in your blood and bones. If we were doing our job right as Jewish parents, you'd be incapable of doing . . . a lot of the things we know very well you do."

"Just because I sometimes eat – "

Her father cut in swiftly. "It's got very little to do with what you eat. Kosher's not the real point at all. Keeping kosher is just a symbol, sometimes of something Jews forget to feel – Jews like us who live in other people's countries."

Other people's countries?

"But isn't Canada our country?"

"No. Not really."

"Why not? *Why not?*"

"It's a Christian country."

There was a moment's silence. Then Lesley burst out, "But there aren't any Jewish countries! Except . . . "

"Except Israel. Exactly. And that's where we're going."

Lesley simply couldn't take it in at first. Israel!

Suddenly her mind began to thaw out of its shock and look at this – could it be a *fact*? Could her father, whom she'd always loved and trusted, really be going to uproot them all from their safe, comfortable, happy life and drag them off to that faraway place where there was always trouble and fighting?

"But – but – I was *born* here! It's my *home!*" she burst out. Her voice wasn't quiet now. "You can't expect me to leave – my house, my street, school – all my friends – Sonia – Lee—"

Each word took her deeper into strange, untrodden

realms of despair, and she began to cry, her voice rising and rising. Her father stood up and came towards her, but she dodged him and ran away to the window.

Through it she could see the garden, with its beautiful fiery maple tree, the hedge she used to hide behind for fun when her father came home, the trim lawn where the couples had danced and necked on her fourteenth birthday, just a month ago . . . Two of her friends came down the street as she stared through a blur of tears, riding their bikes and laughing . . . Safe.

And beyond, the Saskatchewan River, her river that she had played by and looked at and loved and taken for granted all her life, gliding by in the sun as if nothing were happening.

She whirled around and faced her parents. Her face was contorted.

"I'll die if you make me go!" she shouted. "You can't do this to people!" And when her father reached towards her, she struck down his arm. "I don't want to be a Jew if this is what it means. I'm Canadian, do you hear me? I'm *Canadian!*"

"And part of you will always—" began her mother's voice soothingly in the background, but her father cut in.

"It's better if you look ahead now. Our future isn't here. It's in a place where we can be ourselves without fear or favour. We're going to Israel, Lesley. Accept it."

"I won't!" she screamed passionately. "I won't, I won't, I won't!" She heard how it sounded, like a spoiled baby throwing a tantrum, and she saw her mother jump up, but she was beyond control.

A moment later, she was slamming the doors of the room so hard she felt the vibrations all the way up her arms to her shoulders. She left the front door swinging, ran across the main road without looking out for cars, and flung herself down the riverbank to her own secret place. There she fell to the ground and lay crying aloud with bitter incomprehension, rage, and fear.

The bright autumn leaves stuck in her hair as she twisted her head back and forth. Below her, through the trees, the slow, majestic river glinted. Being near it had soothed and cheered her all her life. But now she wept on heedlessly, beyond comfort, as if the end of summer were the end of the world.

THE RED PONY

JOHN STEINBECK

Jody is the son of a rancher, Carl Tiflin. Jody was given a red colt as a gift and though he looked after it well, it took sick and died. Now one of the mares, Nellie, is due to give birth and Jody has been promised the colt when it is born.

THE WINTER FELL SHARPLY. A few preliminary gusty showers, and then a strong steady rain. The hills lost their straw colour and blackened under the water, and the winter streams scrambled noisily down the canyons. The mushrooms and puffballs popped up and the new grass started before Christmas.

But this year Christmas was not the central day to Jody. Some undetermined time in January had become the axis day around which the months swung. When the rains fell, he put Nellie in a box stall and fed her warm food every morning and curried her and brushed her.

The mare was swelling so greatly that Jody became alarmed. "She'll pop wide open," he said to Billy.

Billy laid his strong square hand against Nellie's swollen abdomen. "Feel here," he said quietly. "You can feel it move. I guess it would surprise you if there were twin colts."

"You don't think so?" Jody cried. "You don't think it will be twins, do you, Billy?"

"No, I don't, but it does happen, sometimes."

During the first two weeks of January it rained steadily. Jody spent most of his time, when he wasn't in school, in the box stall with Nellie. Twenty times a day he put his hand on her stomach to feel the colt move. Nellie became more and more gentle and friendly to him. She rubbed her nose on him. She whinnied softly when he walked into the barn.

Carl Tiflin came to the barn with Jody one day. He looked admiringly at the groomed bay coat, and he felt the firm flesh over ribs and shoulders. "You've done a good job," he said to Jody. And this was the greatest praise he knew how to give. Jody was tight with pride for hours afterwards.

The fifteenth of January came, and the colt was not born. And the twentieth came; a lump of fear began to form in Jody's stomach. "Is it all right?" he demanded of Billy.

"Oh, sure,"

And again, "Are you sure it's going to be all right?"

Billy stroked the mare's neck. She swayed her head uneasily. "I told you it wasn't always the same time, Jody. You just have to wait."

When the end of the month arrived with no birth, Jody grew frantic. Nellie was so big that her breath came heavily, and her ears were close together and straight up, as though her head ached. Jody's sleep grew restless, and his dreams confused.

On the night of the second of February he awakened crying. His mother called to him, "Jody, you're dreaming. Wake up and start over again."

But Jody was filled with terror and desolation. He lay quietly a few moments, waiting for his mother to go back to sleep, and then he slipped his clothes on, and crept out in his bare feet.

The night was black and thick. A little misting rain fell. The cypress tree and the bunkhouse loomed and then dropped back into the mist. The barn door screeched as he opened it, a thing it never did in the daytime. Jody went to the rack and found a lantern and a tin box of matches. He lighted the wick and walked down the long straw-covered aisle to Nellie's stall. She was standing up. Her whole body weaved from side to side. Jody called to her, "So, Nellie, so-o, Nellie," but she did not stop her swaying nor look around. When he stepped into the stall and touched her on the shoulder she shivered under his hand. Then Billy Buck's voice came from the hayloft right above the stall.

"Jody, what are you doing?"

Jody started back and turned miserable eyes up towards the nest where Billy was lying in the hay. "Is she all right, do you think?"

"Why sure, I think so."

"You won't let anything happen, Billy, you're sure you won't?"

Billy growled down at him, "I told you I'd call you, and I will. Now you get back to bed and stop worrying that mare. She's got enough to do without you worrying her."

Jody cringed, for he had never heard Billy speak in such a tone. "I only thought I'd come and see," he said. "I woke up."

Billy softened a little then. "Well, you get to bed. I don't want you bothering her. I told you I'd get you a good colt. Get along now."

Jody walked slowly out of the barn. He blew out the lantern and set it in the rack. The blackness of the night, and the chilled mist struck him and enfolded him. He wished he believed everything Billy said as he had before the pony died. It was a moment before his eyes, blinded by the feeble lantern-flame, could make any form of the darkness. The damp ground chilled his bare feet. At the cypress-tree the roosting turkeys chattered a little in alarm, and the two good dogs responded to their duty and came charging out, barking to frighten away the coyotes they thought were prowling under the tree.

As he crept through the kitchen, Jody stumbled over a chair. Carl called from his bedroom, "Who's there? What's the matter there?"

And Mrs Tiflin said sleepily, "What's the matter, Carl?"

The next second Carl came out of the bedroom carrying a candle, and found Jody before he could get into bed. "What are you doing out?"

Jody turned shyly away. "I was down to see the mare."

For a moment anger at being awakened fought with approval in Jody's father. "Listen," he said, finally, "there's not a man in this country that knows more about colts than Billy. You leave it to him."

Words burst out of Jody's mouth: "But the pony died—"

"Don't you go blaming that on him," Carl said sternly. "If Billy can't save a horse, it can't be saved."

Mrs Tiflin called, "Make him clean his feet and go to bed, Carl. He'll be sleepy all day tomorrow."

It seemed to Jody that he had just closed his eyes to try to go to sleep when he was shaken violently by the shoulder. Billy Buck stood beside him, holding a lantern in his hand. "Get up," he said. "Hurry up." He turned and walked quickly out of the room.

Mrs Tiflin called, "What's the matter? Is that you, Billy?"

"Yes, ma'am."

"Is Nellie ready?"

"Yes, ma'am."

"All right, I'll get up and heat some water in case you need it."

Jody jumped into his clothes so quickly that he was out the back door before Billy's swinging lantern was half-way to the barn. There was a rim of dawn on the mountain-tops, but no light had penetrated into the cup of the ranch yet. Jody ran frantically after the lantern and caught up to Billy just as he reached the barn. Billy hung the lantern to a nail on the stallside and took off his blue denim coat. Jody saw that he wore only a sleeveless shirt under it.

Nellie was standing rigid and stiff. While they watched, she crouched. Her whole body was wrung with a spasm. The spasm passed. But in a few moments it started over again, and passed.

Billy muttered nervously, "There's something wrong." His bare hand disappeared. "Oh, Jesus," he said. "It's wrong."

The spasm came again, and this time Billy strained, and the muscles stood out on his arm and shoulder. He heaved strongly, his forehead beaded with perspiration. Nellie cried with pain. Billy was muttering: "It's wrong. I can't turn it. It's way wrong. It's turned all around wrong."

He glared wildly towards Jody. And then his fingers made a careful, careful diagnosis. His cheeks were growing tight and grey. He looked for a long questioning minute at Jody standing back of the stall. Then Billy stepped to the rack under the manure window and picked up a horseshoe hammer with his wet right hand.

"Go outside, Jody," he said.

The boy stood still and stared dully at him.

"Go outside, I tell you. It'll be too late."

Jody didn't move.

Then Billy walked quickly to Nellie's head. He cried, "Turn your face away, damn you, turn your face."

This time Jody obeyed. His head turned sideways. He heard Billy whispering hoarsely in the stall. And then he heard a hollow crunch of bone. Nellie chuckled shrilly. Jody looked back in time to see the hammer rise and fall again on the flat forehead. Then Nellie fell heavily to her side and quivered for a moment.

Billy jumped to the swollen stomach; his big pocket-knife was in his hand. He lifted the skin and drove the knife in. He sawed and ripped at the tough belly. The air filled with the sick odour of warm living entrails. The other horses reared back against their halter chains and squealed and kicked.

Billy dropped the knife. Both of his arms plunged into the terrible ragged hole and dragged out a big, white, dripping bundle. His teeth tore a hole in the covering. A little black head appeared through the tear, and little slick, wet ears. A gurgling breath was drawn, and then another. Billy shucked off the sac and found his knife and cut the string. For a moment he held the little black colt in his arms and looked at it. And then he walked slowly over and laid it in the straw at Jody's feet.

Billy's face and arms and chest were dripping red. His body shivered and his teeth chattered. His voice was gone; he spoke in a throaty whisper. "There's your colt. I promised. And there it is. I had to do it – had to." He stopped and looked over his shoulder into the box stall. "Go get hot water and a sponge," he whispered. "Wash him an' dry him the way his mother would. You'll have to feed him by hand. But there's your colt, the way I promised."

Jody stared stupidly at the wet, panting foal. It stretched

out its chin and tried to raise its head. Its blank eyes were navy blue.

"God damn you," Billy shouted, "will you go now for the water? *Will you go?*"

Then Jody turned and trotted out of the barn into the dawn. He ached from his throat to his stomach. His legs were stiff and heavy. He tried to be glad because of the colt, but the bloody face, and the haunted, tired eyes of Billy Buck hung in the air ahead of him.

OUR FIELD

MRS EWING

THERE WERE FOUR OF US, and three of us had godfathers and godmothers. Three each. Three times three make nine, and not a fairy godmother in the lot. That was what vexed us.

It was very provoking, because we knew so well what we wanted if we had one, and she had given us three wishes each. Three times three make nine. We could have got all we wanted out of nine wishes, and have provided for Perronet into the bargain. It would not have been any good Perronet having wishes all to himself, because he was only a dog.

We never knew who it was that drowned Perronet, but it was Sandy who saved his life and brought him home. It was when he was coming home from school, and he brought Perronet with him. Perronet was not at all nice to look at when we first saw him, though we were very sorry for him. He was wet all over, and his eyes shut, and you could see his ribs, and he looked quite dark and sticky. But when he dried, he dried a lovely yellow, with two black ears like velvet. People sometimes asked us what kind of dog he was, but we never knew, except that he was the nicest possible kind.

When we had got him, we were afraid we were not

going to be allowed to have him. Mother said we could not afford him, because of the tax and his keep. The tax was five shillings, but there wanted nearly a year to the time of paying it. Of course his keep began as soon as he could eat, and that was the very same evening. We were all very miserable, because we were so fond of Perronet – at least, Perronet was not his name then, but he was the same person – and at last it was settled that all three of us would give up sugar, towards saving the expense of his keep, if he might stay. It was hardest for Sandy, because he was particularly fond of sweet things; but then he was particularly fond of Perronet. So we all gave up sugar, and Perronet was allowed to remain.

About the tax, we thought we could save any pennies or half-pennies we got during the year, and it was such a long time to the time for paying, that we should be almost sure to have enough by then. We had not any money at the time, or we should have bought a savings-box; but lots of people save their money in stockings, and we settled that we would. An old stocking would not do, because of the holes, and I had not many good pairs; but we took one of my winter ones to use in the summer, and then we thought we could pour the money into one of my good summer ones when the winter came.

What we most of all wanted a fairy godmother for was about our "homes". There was no kind of play we liked better than playing at houses and new homes. But no matter where we made our "home", it was sure to be disturbed. If it was indoors, and we made a palace under the big table, as soon as ever we had got it nicely divided into rooms according to where the legs came, it was certain to be dinner-time, and people put their feet into it. The nicest house we ever had was in the outhouse; we had it, and kept it quite a secret, for weeks. And then the new load of wood came and covered up everything, our best oyster-shell dinner-service and all.

Anyone can see that it is impossible really to fancy

anything when you are constantly interrupted. You can't have any fun out of a railway train stopping at stations, when they take all your carriages to pieces because the chairs are wanted for tea; any more than you can play properly at Grace Darling in a life-boat, when they say the old cradle is too good to be knocked about in that way. It was always the same. If we wanted to play at Thames Tunnel under the beds, we were not allowed; and the day we did Aladdin in the store-closet, old Jane came and would put away the soap, just when Aladdin could not possibly have got the door of the cave open.

It was one day early in May – a very hot day for the time of year, which had made us rather cross – when Sandy came in about four o'clock, smiling more broadly even than usual, and said to Richard and me: "I've got a fairy godmother, and she's given us a field."

Sandy was very fond of eating, especially sweet things. He used to keep back things from meals to enjoy afterwards, and he almost always had a piece of cake in his pocket. He brought a piece out now, and took a large mouthful, laughing at us with his eyes over the top of it.

"What's the good of a field?" said Richard.

"Splendid houses in it," said Sandy.

"I'm quite tired of fancying homes," said I. "It's no good; we always get turned out."

"It's quite a new place," Sandy continued; "you've never been there," and he took a triumphant bite of the cake.

"How did you get there?" asked Richard.

"The fairy godmother showed me," was Sandy's reply.

There is such a thing as nursery honour. We respected each other's pretendings unless we were very cross, but I didn't disbelieve in his fairy godmother. I only said, "You shouldn't talk with your mouth full," to snub him for making a secret about his field.

Sandy is very good-tempered. He only laughed and said, "Come along. It's much cooler out now. The sun's going down."

He took us along Gipsy Lane. We had been there once or twice, for walks, but not very often, for there was some horrid story about it which rather frightened us. I do not know what it was, but it was a horrid one. Still we had been there, and I knew it quite well. At the end of it there is a stile, by which you go into a field, and at the other end you get over another stile, and find yourself in the high road.

"If this is our field, Sandy," said I, when we got to the first stile, "I'm very sorry, but it really won't do. I know that lots of people come through it. We should never be quiet here."

Sandy laughed. He didn't speak, and he didn't get over the stile; he went through a gate close by it leading into a little sort of bye-lane that was all mud in winter and hard cart-ruts in summer. I had never been up it, but I had seen hay and that sort of thing go in and come out of it.

He went on and we followed him. The ruts were very

disagreeable to walk on, but presently he led us through a
hole in the hedge, and we got into a field. It was a very
bare-looking field, and went rather uphill. There was no
path, but Sandy walked away up it, and we went after
him. There was another hedge at the top, and a stile in it.
It had very rough posts, one much longer than the other,
and the cross-step was gone, but there were two rails, and
we all climbed over. And when we got to the other side,
Sandy leaned against the big post and gave a wave with his
right hand and said, "This is our field."

It sloped down hill, and the hedges round it were rather
high, with awkward branches of blackthorn sticking out
here and there without any leaves, and with the blossom
lying white on the black twigs like snow. There were cowslips all over the field, but they were thicker at the lower
end, which was damp. The great heat of the day was over.
The sun shone still, but it shone low down and made such
splendid shadows that we all walked about with grey
giants at our feet; and it made the bright green of the grass,
and the cowslips down below, and the top of the hedge,
and Sandy's hair, and everything in the sun and the mist
behind the elder bush which was out of the sun, so yellow
– so very yellow – that just for a minute I really believed
about Sandy's godmother, and thought it was a story come
true, and that everything was turning into gold.

But it was only for a minute; of course I know that fairy
tales are not true. But it was a lovely field, and when we
had put our hands to our eyes, and had a good look at it, I
said to Sandy, "I beg your pardon, Sandy, for telling you
not to talk with your mouth full. It is the best field I ever
heard of."

"Sit down," said Sandy, doing the honours; and we all
sat down under the hedge.

"There are violets just behind us," he continued. "Can't
you smell them? But whatever you do, don't tell anybody
of those, or we shan't keep our field to ourselves for a day.
And look here." He had turned over on to his face, and

Richard and I did the same, whilst Sandy fumbled among the bleached grass and brown leaves.

"Hyacinths," said Richard, as Sandy displayed the green tops of them.

"As thick as peas," said Sandy. "This bank will be blue in a few weeks; and fiddle-heads everywhere. There will be no end of ferns. May to any extent -- it's only in bud yet – and there's a wren's nest in there – " At this point he rolled suddenly over on to his back and looked up.

"A lark," he explained; "there was one singing its head off, this morning. I say, Dick, this will be a good field for a kite, won't it? *But wait a bit.*"

After every fresh thing that Sandy showed us in our field, he always finished by saying, *"Wait a bit"*; and that was because there was always something else better still.

"There's a brook at the bottom there," he said, "with lots of fresh-water shrimps. I wonder whether they would boil red. *But wait a bit.* This hedge, you see, has got a very high bank, and it's worn into kind of ledges. I think we could play at 'shops' there – but *wait a bit.*"

"It's almost *too* good, Sandy dear!" said I, as we crossed the field to the opposite hedge.

"The best is to come," said Sandy. "I've a very good mind not to let it out till tomorrow." And to our distraction he sat down in the middle of the field, put his arms round his knees, as if we were playing at "Honey-pots", and rocked himself backwards and forwards with a face of brimming satisfaction.

Neither Richard nor I would have been so mean as to explore on our own account, when the field was Sandy's discovery, but we tried hard to persuade him to show us everything.

He had the most provoking way of laughing and holding his tongue, and he did that now, besides slowly turning all his pockets inside-out into his hands, and mumbling up the crumbs and odd currants, saying "Guess!" between every mouthful.

But when there was not a crumb left in the seams of his pockets, Sandy turned them back, and jumping up, said – "One can only tell a secret once. It's a hollow oak. Come along!"

He ran and we ran, to the other side of Our Field. I had read of hollow oaks, and seen pictures of them, and once I dreamed of one, with a witch inside, but we had never had one to play in. We were nearly wild with delight. It looked all solid from the field, but when we pushed behind, on the hedge side, there was the door, and I crept in, and it smelt of wood, and delicious damp. There could not be a more perfect castle, and though there were no windows in the sides, the light came in from the top, where the polypody hung over like a fringe. Sandy was quite right. It was the very best thing in Our Field.

Perronet was as fond of the field as we were. What he liked were the little birds. At least, I don't know that he liked them, but they were what he chiefly attended to. I think he knew that it was our field, and thought he was the watch-dog of it, and whenever a bird settled down anywhere, he barked at it, and then it flew away, and he ran barking after it till he lost it; and by that time another had settled down, and then Perronet flew at him, and so on, all up and down the hedge. He never caught a bird, and never would let one sit down, if he could see it.

We had all kinds of games in Our Field. Shops – for there were quantities of things to sell – and sometimes I was a moss-merchant, for there were ten different kinds of moss by the brook, and sometimes I was a jeweller, and sold daisy-chains and pebbles, and coral sets made of holly berries, and oak-apple necklaces; and sometimes I kept a flower-shop, and sold nosegays and wreaths, and umbrellas made of rushes. I liked that kind of shop, because I am fond of arranging flowers, and I always make our birthday wreaths. And sometimes I kept a whole lot of shops, and Richard and Sandy bought my things, and paid for them with money made of elder-pith, sliced into rounds. The first shop I kept was to sell cowslips, and Richard and Sandy lived by the brook, and were wine merchants, and made cowslip wine in a tin mug.

The elder-tree was a beauty. In July the cream-coloured flowers were so sweet, we could hardly sit under it, and in the autumn it was covered with berries; but we were always a little disappointed that they never tasted in the least like elderberry syrup. Richard used to make flutes out of the stalks, and one really did work well enough to play tunes on, but it always made Perronet bark.

Richard's every-day cap had a large hole in the top, and when we were in Our Field we always hung it on the top of the tallest of the two stile-posts, to show that we were there; just as the Queen has a flag hung out at Windsor Castle, when she is at home.

We played at castles and houses, and when we were tired of the houses, we pretended to pack up, and went to the seaside for change of air by the brook. Sandy and I took off our shoes and stockings and were bathing-women, and we bathed Perronet; and Richard sat on the bank and was a "tripper", looking at us through a telescope; for when the elder-stems cracked and wouldn't do for flutes, he made them into telescopes. And before we went down to the brook we made jam of hips and haws from the hedge at the top of the field, and put it into acorn cups, and took it with us, that the children might not be short of roly-polies at the seaside.

Whatever we played at we were never disturbed. Birds, and cows, and men and horses ploughing in the distance, do not disturb you at all.

We were very happy that summer: the boys were quite happy, and the only thing that vexed me was thinking of Perronet's tax-money. For months and months went on and we did not save it. Once we got as far as two-pence halfpenny, and then one day Richard came to me and said, "I must have some string for the kite. You might lend me a penny out of Perronet's stocking, till I get some money of

my own."

So I did; and the next day Sandy came and said, "You lent Dick one of Perronet's coppers: I'm sure Perronet would lend me one," and then they said it was ridiculous to leave a half-penny there by itself, so we spent it on acid drops.

It worried me so much at last, that I began to dream horrible dreams about Perronet having to go away because we hadn't saved his tax-money. And then I used to wake up and cry, till the pillow was so wet, I had to turn it. The boys never seemed to mind, but then boys don't think about things; so that I was quite surprised when one day I found Sandy alone in our field with Perronet in his arms, crying, and feeding him with cake; and I found he was crying about the tax-money.

I cannot bear to see boys cry. I would much rather cry myself, and I begged Sandy to leave off, for I said I was quite determined to try and think of something.

It certainly was remarkable that the very next day should be the day when we heard about the flower-show.

It was in school – the village school, for mother could not afford to send us anywhere else – and the schoolmaster rapped on his desk and said, "Silence, children!" and that at the agricultural show there was to be a flower-show this year, and that an old gentleman was going to give prizes to the school-children for window-plants and for the best arranged wild flowers. There were to be nosegays and wreaths, and there was to be a first prize of five shillings, and a second prize of half-a-crown, for the best collection of wild flowers with the names put to them.

"The English names," said the schoolmaster; "and there may be – silence, children! – there may be collections of ferns, or grasses, or mosses to compete, too, for the gentleman wishes to encourage a taste for natural history."

And several of the village children said, "What's that?" and I squeezed Sandy's arm, who was sitting next to me, and whispered "Five shillings!" and the schoolmaster said, "Silence, children!" and I thought I never should have finished my lessons that day for thinking of Perronet's tax-money.

July is not at all a good month for wild flowers; May and June are far better. However, the show was to be in the first week in July.

I said to the boys, "Look here: I'll do a collection of flowers. I know the names, and I can print. It's no good two or three people muddling with arranging flowers; but if you will get me what I want, I shall be very much obliged. If either of you will make another collection, you know there are ten kinds of mosses by the brook; and we have names for them of our own, and they are English. Perhaps they'll do. But everything must come out of Our Field."

The boys agreed, and they were very good. Richard made me a box, rather high at the back. We put sand at the bottom and damped it, and then Feather Moss, lovely clumps of it, and into that I stuck the flowers. They all came out of Our Field. I like to see the grass with flowers, and we had very pretty grasses, and between every bunch of flowers I put a bunch of grass of different kinds. I got all the flowers and all the grasses ready first, and printed the names on pieces of cardboard to stick in with them, and then I arranged them by my eye, and Sandy handed me what I called for, for Richard was busy at the brook making a tray of mosses.

Sandy knew the flowers and the names of them quite as well as I did, of course; we knew everything that lived in Our Field; so when I called, "Ox-eye daisies, cock's-foot grass, labels; meadow-sweet, fox-tail grass, labels; dog-roses, shivering grass, labels" and so on, he gave me the right things, and I had nothing to do but to put the colours that looked best together next to each other, and to make the grass look light, and pull up bits of the moss to show well. And at the very end I put in a label, "All out of Our Field."

I did not like it when it was done; but Richard praised it so much, it cheered me up, and I thought his mosses looked lovely.

The flower-show day was very hot. I did not think it could be hotter anywhere in the world than it was in the field where the show was; but it was hotter in the tent.

We should never have got in at all – for you had to pay at the gate – but they let competitors in free, though not at first. When we got in, there were a lot of grown-up people, and it was very hard work getting along among them, and getting to see the stands with the things on. We kept seeing tickets with "1st Prize" and "2nd Prize", and struggling up; but they were sure to be dahlias in a tray, or fruit that you mightn't eat, or vegetables. The vegetables disappointed us so often, I got to hate them. I don't think I shall ever like very big potatoes (before they are boiled) again, particularly the red ones. It makes me feel sick with heat and anxiety to think of them.

We had struggled slowly all round the tent, and seen all the cucumbers, onions, lettuces, long potatoes, round potatoes, and everything else, when we saw an old gentleman, with spectacles and white hair, standing with two or three ladies. And then we saw three nosegays in jugs, with all the green picked off, and the flowers tied as

tightly together as they would go, and then we saw some prettier ones, and then we saw my collection, and it had got a big label in it marked, "1st Prize", and next to it came Richard's moss-tray, with the Hair-moss and the Pin-cushion-moss, and the Scale-mosses, and a lot of others with names of our own, and it was marked "2nd Prize". And I gripped one of Sandy's arms just as Richard seized the other, and we both cried, "Perronet is paid for!"

There was two-and-sixpence over. We never had such a feast! It was a picnic tea, and we had it in Our Field. I thought Sandy and Perronet would have died of cake, but they were none the worse.

We were very much frightened at first when the old gentleman invited himself; but he would come, and he brought a lot of nuts, and he did get inside the oak, though it is really too small for him.

I don't think there ever was anybody so kind. If he were not a man, I should really and truly believe in Sandy's fairy godmother.

Of course I don't really believe in fairies. I am not so young as that. And I know that Our Field does not exactly belong to us.

I wonder to whom it does belong? Richard says he believes it belongs to the gentleman who lives at the big red house among the trees. But he must be wrong; for we see that gentleman at church every Sunday, but we never saw him in Our Field.

And I don't believe anybody could have such a field of their very own, and never come to see it, from one end of summer to the other.

LION BY MOONLIGHT

RICHARD PARKER

from Lion at Large

STANDING IN THE MOONLIGHT just outside the front gate, the lion looked unusually large. Barry, in his pyjamas, stared at the animal through the glass of his bedroom window and hardly dared to breathe. When he did, the glass misted over and he had to move his head. Perhaps it was the narrowness of the street and the fact that the houses were only one-storey prefabs; the lion looked as big as a horse.

The lion was standing still, looking down towards the end of the road, past the two half-built houses to the orchard beyond. The land dipped suddenly there to the railway, and then flattened out to a series of damp, grassy meadows through which the river wound in smooth wormy loops. There would be a mist over the river, Barry thought. There almost always was at this time of the night.

What time of night? What time was it then? Barry had woken up and got straight out of bed without knowing why he did so. For some reason, he had gone to the window and seen the lion. It was almost as if the creature was waiting for him. Barry turned his head to look at the clock on the chest-of-drawers, but he could not bear to look away from the lion for so long and snatched his eyes away before they had seen what the time was. The lion had not moved.

Barry lifted a hand to the latch to open the window, but before his hand was half-way there the lion swung his head around and stared straight at him. Barry did not dare move, either to complete the action or to withdraw his hand. He could see the lion's nostrils going wide and then narrow, trying to smell him out.

Suddenly the lion trotted towards the gate, three or four steps, then made as if to spring over it. He only raised the front part of his body, however, and put his two front paws on the top of the gate. Barry noticed how large the paws were. One of them stretched across the top of two of the palings that made the gate. The lion shook the little gate and Barry could hear the latch rattling. This frightened him. He had not felt at all afraid before; now he wished he had not got out of bed. He would have liked to jump back in, but he was afraid to move.

The lion crouched two or three times as if he was going to leap over the gate. Then he raised himself and dropped back on all fours on the pavement. After that he did not look quite so big; he was almost hidden behind the gate. Barry could see the end of his tail beyond the little clump of laurels; it twitched from side to side in sharp jerks.

Barry took a soft step backward, away from the window. He felt the edge of the carpet under his heel; also something hard and cold. Without looking down, he knew it was a piece of his Meccano set and that it was a triangular piece called a trunnion. Somehow that was reassuring; he watched the lion with a faint feeling of superiority.

While he was doing this, the lion moved again. He walked along close to the fence, almost out of sight until he reached the corner of the garden. There was no fence next door, for that was where one of the new houses was to be. Instead, there was a rutted track where the builders' trucks turned; the mud had been pushed madly about in the wet weather, and got mixed up with half-bricks, sand, lime and other builders' rubble, and then had dried hard into a number of broken ridges. The lion stopped at the edge of this rough part and sniffed the ground; then he went forward slowly, walking with care on the tops of the hard ridges.

When he reached a heap of sand on the far side of the track, he stood still again with his head raised as if he had heard a sound in the orchard. Then, so quickly that Barry hardly realized what had happened, he bounded clear over the sand and ran down through the trees until the white blossoms and the silver-grey trunks hid him from sight.

Barry waited for a few minutes at the window in case the lion should come back, but somehow he knew he would not. The boy shivered slightly, although he was not at all cold, and wondered what he ought to do. It struck him for the first time that it was not the usual thing for lions to be wandering in the moonlight among the prefabs of Barclay Close. He ought to tell someone of what he had just seen.

He went out of his bedroom and across the hall and then stood with one hand on the handle of his parents' bedroom door. He knew they would both be asleep. What would they do if he woke them up to say he had seen a lion in the road? Would his father get up and get dressed in order to go out and report to the police? The police station was a long way from here. Even the nearest telephone-box was on the other side of the orchard. More than likely, Dad wouldn't be at all pleased at being wakened. He would say, "A lion? Are you sure it wasn't a big dog? A Great Dane or something? Great Danes look pretty much like lions, especially in the dark."

"No, honestly, Dad, it was a lion all right. It had a mane and everything. I saw it when it got up on the garden gate," Barry would say.

"Where is it now?"

"It ran off down the orchard."

Then what? Dad would most probably mumble something about seeing to it in the morning, and to get back in bed before you catch cold, or something of the sort.

Barry let his hand slip off the door handle and turned back to his bedroom. It would be a better idea to wait until morning. As he climbed back into bed, he decided he would wake early and catch his father before he went to work. He could go past the police station, and it would only take him a minute to go in and report to the policeman on duty. It would not make him late for work. He could even leave a minute or two earlier than usual to make sure of not being late.

Unfortunately when Barry did wake up the following morning his father had already left for work.

"Get up now and you won't have to rush your breakfast," his mother said.

Barry jumped straight out of bed. "Mum, is Dad up?"

"Of course he is. And gone to work."

"But I had something important to tell him."

"It'll have to wait till this evening, then," said his mother, already half-way out of the room.

"Wait a minute—"

"I've got the bacon on; I can't," she said. "Put clean socks on; I've left them on your chair."

Barry pursued her to the kitchen. "But, Mum, listen," he said. "I saw a lion out of the window last night. Just wandering about in the road it was. Then it went right down through the orchard."

"Oh really, Barry," said his mother. "Look at you, still in your pyjamas. Go and get dressed this very minute."

"But, Mum, didn't you hear what I said?"

"Get your clothes on first. Then I'll listen," said his mother.

Barry went back to his bedroom. He pulled off his pyjama jacket and threw it as hard as he could on the floor.

Then he thumped the bed with his clenched fists eight or nine times. After that he felt better and got dressed. He made his bed and went into the other room for breakfast. He did not say anything else to his mother until they were both sitting at the table.

"Mum," he said, "you didn't hear what I said about last night, did you?"

"No. What did you say?"

"Well, I woke up in the night, you see—"

"I knew you would," said his mother. "You had far too much supper."

"Oh, Mum. *Please!*"

"Well, go on, then."

Barry told his mother exactly what had happened and what he had seen out of the bedroom window. His mother went on eating for a moment, and then she said, "Do you want another slice of bread?"

"Yes," said Barry. "I mean, no."

"Well, make up your mind."

"But what do you think about it, Mum?"

"About what?"

"About the lion," said Barry. "I've just been telling you!"

"I know, and you don't have to shout at me."

"But you haven't said what you think."

"What do you expect me to say? It must have been very exciting for you. Was it a very big lion?"

"I thought so at first, but that was probably just the way the moon was shining. Afterwards it seemed about the usual size."

"I see," said Barry's mother. "Just an ordinary lion. With a mane?"

"Of course it had a mane," said Barry. "Otherwise it would have been a lioness."

"You're dropping marmalade on the cloth," she said. "Do try to be careful; it was clean only yesterday."

Barry scraped up the marmalade with his knife.

"But don't you think it was exciting?" he cried.

"Well, I said so, didn't I?"

"Yes, but you don't look excited."

Barry's mother laughed. "You are a funny boy. What did you expect me to do? Scream? Faint? Throw a fit?"

"I thought you might want to phone the police or something," said Barry. "That's why I wanted to tell Dad; he could have gone into the station on his way to work."

"Oh, Barry," his mother said, smiling. "Really!"

Barry knew what that meant. "But I did see a lion," he said. "Cross my heart. I really and truly did. I'm not making it up."

"Of course you saw one," she said, soothingly. "But it couldn't have been a real one, could it? It must have been a dream. Now do be sensible. A big boy almost ten—"

"I don't see what being almost ten has got to do with it," cried Barry angrily. "At least, I'm old enough to know when I've seen something and when I haven't. How do you know whether it was a dream or not? You weren't there. You were asleep."

"Now you're being rude," said his mother sharply.

"Well, it's enough to make anybody rude," said Barry.

"I think we'd better say no more about it," said his mother, getting up and beginning to clear the table.

"But that's not fair," Barry cried. "Look, I'll prove I'm telling the truth. I think you're being absolutely mean—"

"Barry!" said his mother sharply. "You're being very childish. I think the best thing you can do is to go into your bedroom for ten minutes and calm down. When you feel like coming out and apologizing for being so rude to me—"

Barry did not wait to hear any more, but ran into his bedroom and slammed the door behind him. For a few minutes he walked angrily up and down beside his bed, then he began to feel sorry for himself and imagine himself hurt in some way, so that his mother would be sorry for being so unjust to him. Then he got tired of walking up and down, and he sat on the edge of his bed and sulked.

It was while he was sitting like this, with his chin in his hands that he suddenly noticed something odd. His clock was not on the chest-of-drawers at all. In fact, now he came to think of it, he had been using the clock in the shed the day before and had forgotten to bring it in again. Yet he could have sworn it was on the chest last night. He remembered turning from the window to see the time by it. And if he was wrong about the clock, he could be wrong about the lion.

Suddenly he felt as if he had been plunged into boiling water; every part of his body felt hot and red with embarrassment. Suppose his mother was right after all. Suppose it had been a dream. He did have some pretty powerful dreams sometimes. He jumped off the bed and went to stand by the window in dreadful doubt. It was all very well to say you could prove something, but in fact how could you prove it? The lion wasn't there now, that was certain. In fact, there was a red milk truck just where he had first seen the lion – or dreamed he had seen it.

Everything outside, except the milk truck of course, looked just the same as it had in the night, but that did not prove anything. You often dreamed of things as they were. He stepped back from the window, and then, feeling the edge of the carpet under the heel of his shoe, he looked down. Lying there next to his foot was a triangular piece of Meccano. A piece called a trunnion.

DADDY-LONG-LEGS

JEAN WEBSTER

*Jerusha Abbott, seventeen, is an orphan from the John Grier Home.
Now she has been selected to be sent to college where her fees will be
paid by one of the trustees of the John Grier Home. He wishes to
remain anonymous, though Jerusha once caught a glimpse of him. In
return for her fees being paid, Jerusha must write to her benefactor
every month.*

215 FERGUSSEN HALL
September 24th

DEAR KIND-TRUSTEE-*Who-Sends-Orphans-to-College,*
Here I am! I travelled yesterday for four hours in
a train. It's a funny sensation, isn't it? I never rode
in one before.

College is the biggest, most bewildering place – I get lost
whenever I leave my room. I will write you a description
later when I'm feeling less muddled; also I will tell you
about my lessons. Classes don't begin until Monday
morning, and this is Saturday night. But I wanted to write
a letter first just to get acquainted.

It seems queer to be writing letters to somebody you
don't know. It seems queer for me to be writing letters at
all – I've never written more than three or four in my life,
so please overlook it if these are not a model kind.

196

Before leaving yesterday morning, Mrs Lippett and I had a very serious talk. She told me how to behave all the rest of my life, and especially how to behave toward the kind gentleman who is doing so much for me. I must take care to be Very Respectful.

But how can one be very respectful to a person who wishes to be called John Smith? Why couldn't you have picked out a name with a little personality? I might as well write letters to Dear Hitching-Post or Dear Clothes-Prop.

I have been thinking about you a great deal this summer; having somebody to take an interest in me after all these years makes me feel as though I had found a sort of family. It seems as though I belonged to somebody now, and it's a very comfortable sensation. I must say, however, that when I think about you, my imagination has very little to work upon. There are just three things that I know:

I. You are tall.
II. You are rich.
III. You hate girls.

I suppose I might call you Dear Mr Girl-Hater. Only that's rather insulting to me. Or Dear Mr Rich-Man, but that's insulting to you, as though money were the only important thing about you. Besides, being rich is such a very external quality. Maybe you won't stay rich all your life; lots of very clever men get smashed up in Wall Street. But at least you will stay tall all your life! So I've decided to call you Dear Daddy-Long-Legs. I hope you won't mind. It's just a private pet name – we won't tell Mrs Lippett.

The ten o'clock bell is going to ring in two minutes. Our day is divided into sections by bells. We eat and sleep and study by bells. It's very enlivening; I feel like a fire horse all of the time. There it goes! Lights out. Good night.

Observe with what precision I obey rules – due to my training in the John Grier Home.

Yours most respectfully,
JERUSHA ABBOTT

197

To Mr Daddy-Long-Legs Smith
October 1st

Dear Daddy-Long-Legs,

I love college and I love you for sending me – I'm very, *very* happy, and so excited every moment of the time that I can scarcely sleep. You can't imagine how different it is from the John Grier Home. I never dreamed there was such a place in the world. I'm feeling sorry for everybody who isn't a girl and who can't come here; I am sure the college you attended when you were a boy couldn't have been so nice.

My room is up in a tower that used to be the contagious ward before they built the new infirmary. There are three other girls on the same floor of the tower – a Senior who wears spectacles and is always asking us please to be a little more quiet, and two Freshmen named Sallie McBride and Julia Rutledge Pendleton. Sallie has red hair and a turn-up nose and is quite friendly; Julia comes from one of the first families in New York and hasn't noticed me yet. They room together and the Senior and I have singles. Usually Freshmen can't get singles; they are very scarce, but I got one without even asking. I suppose the registrar didn't think it would be right to ask a properly brought-up girl to room with a foundling. You see there are advantages!

My room is on the north-west corner with two windows and a view. After you've lived in a ward for eighteen years with twenty room-mates, it is restful to be alone. This is the first chance I've ever had to get acquainted with Jerusha Abbott. I think I'm going to like her.

Do you think you are?

Tuesday

They are organising the Freshman basketball team and

there's just a chance that I shall get in it. I'm little of course, but terribly quick and wiry and tough. While the others are hopping about in the air, I can dodge under their feet and grab the ball. It's loads of fun practising – out in the athletic field in the afternoon with the trees all red and yellow and the air full of the smell of burning leaves, and everybody laughing and shouting. These are the happiest girls I ever saw – and I am the happiest of all!

I meant to write a long letter and tell you all the things I'm learning (Mrs Lippett said you wanted to know), but 7th hour has just rung, and in ten minutes I'm due at the athletic field in gymnasium clothes. Don't you hope I'll get in the team?

> Yours always
> JERUSHA ABBOTT

P.S. (9 o'clock)

Sallie McBride just poked her head in at my door. This is what she said:

"I'm so homesick that I simply can't stand it. Do you feel that way?"

I smiled a little and said no, I thought I could pull through. At least homesickness is one disease that I've escaped! I never heard of anybody being asylum-sick, did you?

October 10th

Dear Daddy-Long-Legs,
Did you ever hear of Michael Angelo?

He was a famous artist who lived in Italy in the Middle Ages. Everybody in English Literature seemed to know about him, and the whole class laughed because I thought he was an archangel. He sounds like an archangel, doesn't he? The trouble with college is that you are expected to know such a lot of things you've never learned. It's very embarrassing at times. But now, when the girls talk about things that I never heard of, I just keep still and look them up in the encyclopedia.

I made an awful mistake the first day. Somebody mentioned Maurice Maeterlinck, and I asked if she was a Freshman. That joke has gone all over college. But anyway, I'm just as bright in class as any of the others – and brighter than some of them!

Do you care to know how I've furnished my room? It's a symphony in brown and yellow. The wall was tinted buff, and I've bought yellow denim curtains and cushions and a mahogany desk (second-hand for three dollars) and a rattan chair and a brown rug with an ink spot in the middle. I stand the chair over the spot.

The windows are up high; you can't look out from an ordinary seat. But I unscrewed the looking-glass from the back of the bureau, upholstered the top and moved it up against the window. It's just the right height for a window seat. You pull out the drawers like steps and walk up. Very comfortable!

Sallie McBride helped me choose the things at the Senior auction. She has lived in a house all her life and knows about furnishing. You can't imagine what fun it is to shop and pay with a real five-dollar bill and get some change – when you've never had more than a few cents in your life. I assure you, Daddy dear, I do appreciate that allowance.

Sallie is the most entertaining person in the world – and Julia Rutledge Pendleton the least so. It's queer what a mixture the registrar can make in the matter of room-mates. Sallie thinks everything is funny – even flunking – and Julia is bored at everything. She never makes the slightest effort to be amiable. She believes that if you are a Pendleton, that fact alone admits you to heaven without any further examination. Julia and I were born to be enemies.

And now I suppose you've been waiting very impatiently to hear what I am learning?

I. *Latin*: Second Punic war. Hannibal and his forces

pitched camp at Lake Trasimenus last night. They prepared an ambuscade for the Romans, and a battle took place at the fourth watch this morning. Romans in retreat.

II. *French*: 24 pages of the "Three Musketeers" and third conjugation, irregular verbs.

III. *Geometry*: Finished cylinders; now doing cones.

IV. *English*: Studying exposition. My style improves daily in clearness and brevity.

V. *Physiology*: Reached the digestive system. Bile and the pancreas next time.

Yours, on the way to being educated.

    JERUSHA ABBOTT

P.S. I hope you never touch alcohol, Daddy? It does dreadful things to your liver.

Wednesday

Dear Daddy-Long-Legs,
I've changed my name.

I'm still "Jerusha" in the catalogue, but I'm "Judy" everywhere else. It's really too bad, isn't it, to have to give yourself the only pet name you ever had? I didn't quite make up the Judy though. That's what Freddie Perkins used to call me before he could talk plainly.

I wish Mrs Lippett would use a little more ingenuity about choosing babies' names. She gets the last names out of the telephone book – you'll find Abbott on the first page – and she picks the Christian names up anywhere; she got Jerusha from a tombstone. I've always hated it; but I rather like Judy. It's such a silly name. It belongs to the kind of girl I'm not – a sweet little blue-eyed thing, petted and spoiled by all the family, who romps her way through life without any cares. Wouldn't it be nice to be like that? Whatever faults I may have, no one can ever accuse me of having been spoiled by my family! But it's great fun to pretend I've been. In the future please always address me as Judy.

Do you want to know something? I have three pairs of kid gloves. I've had kid mittens before from the Christmas tree, but never real kid gloves with five fingers. I take them out and try them on every little while. It's all I can do not to wear them to classes.

(Dinner bell. Goodbye.)

Friday

What do you think, Daddy? The English instructor said that my last paper shows an unusual amount of originality. She did, truly. Those were her words. It doesn't seem possible, does it, considering the eighteen years of training that I've had? The aim of the John Grier Home (as you doubtless know and heartily approve of) is to turn the

ANY ORPHAN

Rear Elevation Front Elevation

ninety-seven orphans into ninety-seven twins.

The unusual artistic ability which I exhibit was developed at an early age through drawing chalk pictures of Mrs Lippett on the woodshed door.

I hope that I don't hurt your feelings when I criticise the home of my youth? But you have the upper hand, you

know, for if I become too impertinent, you can always stop payment of your cheques. That isn't a very polite thing to say – but you can't expect me to have any manners; a foundling asylum isn't a young ladies' finishing school.

You know, Daddy, it isn't the work that is going to be hard in college. It's the play. Half the time I don't know what the girls are talking about; their jokes seem to relate to a past that every one but me has shared. I'm a foreigner in the world and I don't understand the language. It's a miserable feeling. I've had it all my life. At the high school the girls would stand in groups and just look at me. I was queer and different and everybody knew it. I could *feel* "John Grier Home" written on my face. And then a few charitable ones would make a point of coming up and saying something polite. *I hated every one of them* – the charitable ones most of all.

Nobody here knows that I was brought up in an asylum. I told Sallie McBride that my mother and father were dead, and that a kind old gentleman was sending me to college – which is entirely true so far as it goes. I don't want you to think I am a coward, but I do want to be like the other girls, and that Dreadful Home looming over my childhood is the one great big difference. If I can turn my back on that and shut out the remembrance, I think I might be just as desirable as any other girl. I don't believe there's any real, underneath difference, do you?

Anyway, Sallie McBride likes me!

> Yours ever,
> JUDY ABBOTT
> (Née Jerusha)

Saturday morning

I've just been reading this letter over and it sounds pretty un-cheerful. But can't you guess that I have a special topic due Monday morning and a review in geometry and a very sneezy cold?

Sunday

I forgot to post this yesterday, so I will add an indignant postscript. We had a bishop this morning, and *what do you think he said*?

"The most beneficent promise made us in the Bible is this, 'The poor ye have always with you.' They were put here in order to keep us charitable."

The poor, please observe, being a sort of useful domestic animal. If I hadn't grown into such a perfect lady, I should have gone up after service and told him what I thought.

October 25th

Dear Daddy-Long-Legs,

I'm in the basketball team and you ought to see the bruise on my left shoulder. It's blue and mahogany with little streaks of orange. Julia Pendleton tried for the team, but she didn't get in. Hooray!

You can see what a mean disposition I have.

College gets nicer and nicer. I like the girls and the teachers and the classes and the campus and the things to eat. We have ice-cream twice a week and we never have corn-meal mush.

You only wanted to hear from me once a month, didn't you? And I've been peppering you with letters every few days! But I've been so excited about all these new adventures that I *must* talk to somebody; and you're the only one I know. Please excuse my exuberance; I'll settle pretty soon. If my letters bore you, you can always toss them into the waste-basket. I promise not to write another till the middle of November.

Yours most loquaciously,
JUDY ABBOTT

PRESIDENT CLEVELAND, WHERE ARE YOU?

ROBERT CORMIER

THAT WAS THE AUTUMN of the cowboy cards – Buck Jones and Tom Tyler and Hoot Gibson and especially Ken Maynard. The cards were available in those five-cent packages of gum: pink sticks, three together, covered with a sweet white powder. You couldn't blow bubbles with that particular gum, but it couldn't have mattered less. The cowboy cards were important – the pictures of those rock-faced men with eyes of blue steel.

On those wind-swept, leaf-tumbling afternoons we gathered after school on the sidewalk in front of Lemire's Drugstore, across from St Jude's Parochial School, and we swapped and bargained and matched for the cards. Because a Ken Maynard serial was playing at the Globe every Saturday afternoon, he was the most popular cowboy of all, and one of his cards was worth at least ten of any other kind. Rollie Tremaine had a treasure of thirty or so, and he guarded them jealously. He'd match you for the other cards, but he risked his Ken Maynards only when the other kids threatened to leave him out of the competition altogether.

You could almost hate Rollie Tremaine. In the first place, he was the only son of Auguste Tremaine, who operated the Uptown Dry Goods Store, and he did not live in a tenement but in a big white birthday cake of a house on Laurel Street. He was too fat to be effective in the football games between the Frenchtown Tigers and the North Side Knights, and he made us constantly aware of the jingle of coins in his pockets. He was able to stroll into Lemire's and casually select a quarter's worth of cowboy cards while the rest of us watched, aching with envy.

Once in a while I earned a nickel or dime by running errands or washing windows for blind old Mrs Belander, or by finding pieces of copper, brass, and other valuable metals at the dump and selling them to the junkman. The coins clutched in my hand, I would race to Lemire's to buy a cowboy card or two, hoping that Ken Maynard would stare boldly out at me as I opened the pack. At one time, before a disastrous matching session with Roger Lussier (my best friend, except where the cards were involved), I owned five Ken Maynards and considered myself a millionaire, of sorts.

One week I was particularly lucky; I had spent two afternoons washing floors for Mrs Belander and received a quarter. Because my father had worked a full week at the shop, where a rush order for fancy combs had been received, he allotted my brothers and sisters and me an extra dime along with the usual ten cents for the Saturday-afternoon movie. Setting aside the movie fare, I found myself with a bonus of thirty-five cents, and I then planned to put Rollie Tremaine to shame the following Monday afternoon.

Monday was the best day to buy the cards because the candy man stopped at Lemire's every Monday morning to deliver the new assortments. There was nothing more exciting in the world than a fresh batch of card boxes. I rushed home from school that day and hurriedly changed my clothes, eager to set off for the store. As I burst through the doorway, letting the screen door slam behind me, my brother Armand blocked my way.

He was fourteen, three years older than I, and a freshman at Monument High School. He had recently become a stranger to me in many ways – indifferent to such matters as cowboy cards and the Frenchtown Tigers – and he carried himself with a mysterious dignity that was fractured now and then when his voice began shooting off in all directions like some kind of vocal fireworks.

"Wait a minute, Jerry," he said. "I want to talk to you." He motioned me out of earshot of my mother, who was busy supervising the usual after-school skirmish in the kitchen.

I sighed with impatience. In recent months Armand had become a figure of authority, siding with my father and mother occasionally. As the oldest son he sometimes took advantage of his age and experience to issue rules and regulations.

"How much money have you got?" he whispered.

"You in some kind of trouble?" I asked, excitement rising in me as I remembered the blackmail plot of a movie at the Globe a month before.

He shook his head in annoyance. "Look," he said, "it's Pa's birthday tomorrow. I think we ought to chip in and buy him something . . . "

I reached into my pocket and caressed the coins. "Here," I said carefully, pulling out a nickel. "If we all give a nickel we should have enough to buy him something pretty nice."

He regarded me with contempt. "Rita already gave me fifteen cents, and I'm throwing in a quarter. Albert handed over a dime – all that's left of his birthday money. Is that all you can do – a nickel?"

"Aw, come on," I protested. "I haven't got a single Ken Maynard left, and I was going to buy some cards this

afternoon."

"Ken Maynard!" he snorted. "Who's more important – him or your father?"

His question was unfair because he knew that there was no possible choice – "my father" had to be the only answer. My father was a huge man who believed in the things of the spirit, although my mother often maintained that the spirits he believed in came in bottles. He had worked at the Monument Comb Shop since the age of fourteen; his booming laugh – or grumble – greeted us each night when he returned from the factory. A steady worker when the shop had enough work, he quickened with gaiety on Friday nights and weekends, a bottle of beer at his elbow, and he was fond of making long speeches about the good things in life. In the middle of the Depression, for instance, he paid cash for a piano, of all things, and insisted that my twin sisters, Yolande and Yvette, take lessons once a week.

I took a dime from my pocket and handed it to Armand.

"Thanks, Jerry," he said. "I hate to take your last cent."

"That's all right," I replied, turning away and consoling myself with the thought that twenty cents was better than nothing at all.

When I arrived at Lemire's I sensed disaster in the air. Roger Lussier was kicking disconsolately at a tin can in the gutter, and Rollie Tremaine sat sullenly on the steps in front of the store.

"Save your money," Roger said. He had known about my plans to splurge on the cards.

"What's the matter?" I asked.

"There's no more cowboy cards," Rollie Tremaine said. "The company's not making any more."

"They're going to have President cards," Roger said, his face twisting with disgust. He pointed to the store window. "Look!"

A placard in the window announced: "Attention, Boys. Watch for the New Series. Presidents of the United States. Free in Each 5-Cent Package of Caramel Chew."

"President cards?" I asked, dismayed.

I read on. "Collect a Complete Set and Receive an Official Imitation Major League Baseball Glove, Embossed with Lefty Grove's Autograph."

Glove or no glove, who could become excited about Presidents, of all things?

Rollie Tremaine stared at the sign. "Benjamin Harrison, for crying out loud," he said. "Why would I want Benjamin Harrison when I've got twenty-two Ken Maynards?"

I felt the warmth of guilt creep over me. I jingled the coins in my pocket, but the sound was hollow. No more Ken Maynards to buy.

"I'm going to buy a Mr Goodbar," Rollie Tremaine decided.

I was without appetite, indifferent even to a Baby Ruth, which was my favourite. I thought of how I had betrayed Armand and, worst of all, my father.

"I'll see you after supper," I called over my shoulder to Roger as I hurried away towards home. I took the shortcut behind the church, although it involved leaping over a tall wooden fence, and I zigzagged recklessly through Mr Thibodeau's garden, trying to outrace my guilt. I pounded up the steps and into the house, only to learn that Armand had already taken Yolande and Yvette uptown to shop for the birthday present.

I pedalled my bike furiously through the streets, ignoring the indignant horns of automobiles as I sliced through the traffic. Finally I saw Armand and my sisters emerge from the Monument Men's Shop. My heart sank when I spied the long, slim package that Armand was holding.

"Did you buy the present yet?" I asked, although I knew it was too late.

"Just now. A blue tie," Armand said. "What's the matter?"

"Nothing," I replied, my chest hurting.

He looked at me for a long moment. At first his eyes were hard, but then they softened. He smiled at me, almost sadly, and touched my arm. I turned away from him because I felt naked and exposed.

"It's all right," he said gently. "Maybe you've learned something." The words were gentle, but they held a curious dignity, the dignity remaining even when his voice suddenly cracked on the last syllable.

I wondered what was happening to me, because I did not know whether to laugh or cry.

Sister Angela was amazed when, a week before Christmas vacation, everybody in the class submitted a history essay worthy of a high mark – in some cases as high as A-minus. (Sister Angela did not believe that anyone in the world ever deserved an A.) She never learned – or at least she never let on that she knew – we all had become experts on the Presidents because of the cards we purchased at Lemire's. Each card contained a picture of a President, and on the reverse side, a summary of his career. We looked at those cards so often that the biographies imprinted themselves on our minds without effort. Even our street-corner conversations were filled with such information as the fact that James Madison was called "The Father of the Constitution," or that John Adams had intended to become a minister.

The President cards were a roaring success and the cowboy cards were quickly forgotten. In the first place we did not receive gum with the cards, but a kind of chewy caramel. The caramel could be tucked into a corner of your mouth, bulging your cheek in much the same manner as wads of tobacco bulged the mouths of baseball stars. In the second place the competition for collecting the cards was fierce and frustrating – fierce because everyone was intent on being the first to send away for a baseball glove and frustrating because although there were only thirty-two Presidents, including Franklin Delano Roosevelt, the variety at Lemire's was at a minimum. When the deliveryman left the boxes of cards at the store each Monday, we often discovered that one entire box was devoted to a single President – two weeks in a row the boxes contained nothing but Abraham Lincolns. One week Roger Lussier and I were the heroes of Frenchtown. We journeyed on our bicycles to the North Side, engaged three boys in a matching bout and returned with five new Presidents, including Chester Alan Arthur, who up to that time had been missing.

Perhaps to sharpen our desire, the card company sent a sample glove to Mr Lemire, and it dangled orange and sleek, in the window. I was half sick with longing, thinking of my old glove at home, which I had inherited from Armand. But Rollie Tremaine's desire for the glove

212

outdistanced my own. He even got Mr Lemire to agree to give the glove in the window to the first person to get a complete set of cards, so that precious time wouldn't be wasted waiting for the postman.

We were delighted at Rollie Tremaine's frustration, especially since he was only a substitute player for the Tigers. Once after spending fifty cents on cards – all of which turned out to be Calvin Coolidge – he threw them to the ground, pulled some dollar bills out of his pocket and said, "The heck with it. I'm going to buy a glove!"

"Not that glove," Roger Lussier said. "Not a glove with Lefty Grove's autograph. Look what it says at the bottom of the sign."

We all looked, although we knew the words by heart: "This Glove Is Not For Sale Anywhere."

Rollie Tremaine scrambled to pick up the cards from the sidewalk, pouting more than ever. After that he was quietly obsessed with the Presidents, hugging the cards

close to his chest and refusing to tell us how many more he needed to complete his set.

I too was obsessed with the cards, because they had become things of comfort in a world that had suddenly grown dismal. After Christmas a layoff at the shop had thrown my father out of work. He received no paycheque for four weeks, and the only income we had was from Armand's after-school job at the Blue and White Grocery Store – a job he lost finally when business dwindled as the layoff continued.

Although we had enough food and clothing – my father's credit had always been good, a matter of pride with him – the inactivity made my father restless and irritable. He did not drink any beer at all, and laughed loudly, but not convincingly, after gulping down a glass of water and saying, "Lent came early this year." The twins fell sick and went to the hospital to have their tonsils removed. My father was confident that he would return to work eventually and pay off his debts, but he seemed to age before our eyes.

When orders again were received at the comb shop and he returned to work, another disaster occurred, although I was the only one aware of it. Armand fell in love.

I discovered his situation by accident, when I happened to pick up a piece of paper that had fallen to the floor in the bedroom he and I shared. I frowned at the paper, puzzled.

"Dear Sally, When I look into your eyes the world stands still . . ."

The letter was snatched from my hands before I finished reading it.

"What's the big idea, snooping around?" Armand asked, his face crimson. "Can't a guy have any privacy?"

He had never mentioned privacy before. "It was on the floor," I said. "I didn't know it was a letter. Who's Sally?"

He flung himself across the bed. "You tell anybody and I'll muckalize you," he threatened. "Sally Knowlton."

Nobody in Frenchtown had a name like Knowlton.

"A girl from the North Side?" I asked, incredulous.

He rolled over and faced me, anger in his eyes, and a kind of despair too.

"What's the matter with that? Think she's too good for me?" he asked. "I'm warning you, Jerry, if you tell anybody . . ."

"Don't worry," I said. Love had no particular place in my life; it seemed an unnecessary waste of time. And a girl from the North Side was so remote that for all practical purposes she did not exist. But I was curious. "What are you writing her a letter for? Did she leave town, or something?"

"She hasn't left town," he answered. "I wasn't going to send it. I just felt like writing to her."

I was glad that I had never become involved with love – love that brought desperation to your eyes, that caused you to write letters you did not plan to send. Shrugging with indifference, I began to search in the closet for the old baseball glove. I found it on the shelf, under some old sneakers. The webbing was torn and the padding gone. I thought of the sting I would feel when a sharp grounder slapped into the glove, and I winced.

"You tell anybody about me and Sally and I'll—"

"I know. You'll muckalize me."

I did not divulge his secret and often shared his agony, particularly when he sat at the supper table and left my mother's special butterscotch pie untouched. I had never realised before how terrible love could be. But my compassion was short-lived because I had other things to worry about: report cards due at Eastertime; the loss of income from old Mrs Belander, who had gone to live with a daughter in Boston; and, of course, the Presidents.

Because a stalemate had been reached, the President cards were the dominant force in our lives – mine, Roger Lussier's and Rollie Tremaine's. For three weeks, as the baseball season approached, each of us had a complete set – complete except for one President, Grover Cleveland.

Each time a box of cards arrived at the store we hurriedly bought them (as hurriedly as our funds allowed) and tore off the wrappers, only to be confronted by James Monroe or Martin Van Buren or someone else. But never Grover Cleveland, never the man who had been the twenty-second *and* the twenty-fourth President of the United States. We argued about Grover Cleveland. Should he be placed between Chester Alan Arthur and Benjamin Harrison as the twenty-second President or did he belong between Benjamin Harrison and William McKinley as the twenty-fourth President? Was the card company playing fair? Roger Lussier brought up a horrifying possibility – did we need *two* Grover Clevelands to complete the set?

Indignant, we stormed Lemire's and protested to the harassed storeowner, who had long since vowed never to stock a new series. Muttering angrily, he searched his bills and receipts for a list of rules.

"All right," he announced. "Says here you only need one Grover Cleveland to finish the set. Now get out, all of you, unless you've got money to spend."

Outside the store, Rollie Tremaine picked up an empty tobacco tin and scaled it across the street. "Boy," he said. "I'd give five dollars for a Grover Cleveland."

When I returned home I found Armand sitting on the piazza steps, his chin in his hands. His mood of dejection mirrored my own, and I sat down beside him. We did not say anything for a while.

"Want to throw the ball around?" I asked.

He sighed, not bothering to answer.

"You sick?" I asked.

He stood up and hitched up his trousers, pulled at his ear and finally told me what the matter was – there was a big dance next week at the high school, the Spring Promenade, and Sally had asked him to be her escort.

I shook my head at the folly of love. "Well, what's so bad about that?"

"How can I take Sally to a fancy dance?" he asked

desperately. "I'd have to buy her a corsage . . . And my shoes are practically falling apart. Pa's got too many worries now to buy me new shoes or give me money for flowers for a girl."

I nodded in sympathy. "Yeah," I said. "Look at me. Baseball time is almost here, and all I've got is that old glove. And no Grover Cleveland card yet . . . "

"Grover Cleveland?" he asked. "They've got some of those up on the North Side. Some kid was telling me there's a store that's got them. He says they're looking for Warren G. Harding."

"Holy Smoke!" I said. "I've got an extra Warren G. Harding!" Pure joy sang in my veins. I ran to my bicycle, swung into the seat – and found that the front tyre was flat.

"I'll help you fix it," Armand said.

Within half an hour I was at the North Side Drugstore, where several boys were matching cards on the sidewalk. Silently but blissfully I shouted: President Grover Cleveland, here I come!

After Armand had left for the dance, all dressed up as if it were Sunday, the small green box containing the corsage under his arm, I sat on the railing of the piazza, letting my feet dangle. The neighbourhood was quiet because the Frenchtown Tigers were at the Daggett's Field, practising for the first baseball game of the season.

I thought of Armand and the ridiculous expression on his face when he'd stood before the mirror in the bedroom. I'd avoided looking at his new black shoes. "Love," I muttered.

Spring had arrived in a sudden stampede of apple blossoms and fragrant breezes. Windows had been thrown open and dust mops had banged on the sills all day long as the women busied themselves with housecleaning. I was puzzled by my lethargy. Wasn't spring supposed to make everything bright and gay?

217

I turned at the sound of footsteps on the stairs. Roger Lussier greeted me with a sour face.

"I thought you were practising with the Tigers," I said.

"Rollie Tremaine," he said. "I just couldn't stand him." He slammed his fist against the railing. "Jeez, why did *he* have to be the one to get a Grover Cleveland? You should see him showing off. He won't let anybody even touch that glove . . ."

I felt like Benedict Arnold and knew that I had to confess what I had done.

"Roger," I said, "I got a Grover Cleveland card up on the North Side. I sold it to Rollie Tremaine for five dollars."

"Are you crazy?" he asked.

"I needed that five dollars. It was an – an emergency."

"Boy!" he said, looking down at the ground and shaking his head. "What did you have to do a thing like that for?"

I watched him as he turned away and began walking down the stairs.

"Hey, Roger!" I called.

He squinted up at me as if I were a stranger, someone he'd never seen before.

"What?" he asked, his voice flat.

"I had to do it," I said. "Honest."

He didn't answer. He headed towards the fence, searching for the board we had loosened to give us a secret passage.

I thought of my father and Armand and Rollie Tremaine and Grover Cleveland and wished that I could go away someplace far away. But there was no place to go.

Roger found the loose slat in the fence and slipped through. I felt betrayed: weren't you supposed to feel good when you did something fine and noble?

A moment later two hands gripped the top of the fence and Roger's face appeared. "Was it a real emergency?" he yelled.

"A real one!" I called. "Something important!"

His face dropped from sight and his voice reached me

across the yard: "All right."

"See you tomorrow!" I yelled.

I swung my legs over the railing again. The gathering dusk began to soften the sharp edges of the fence, the rooftops, the distant church steeple. I sat there a long time, waiting for the good feeling to come.

THE GOLDEN DARTERS

ELIZABETH WINTHROP

I WAS TWELVE YEARS OLD when my father started tying flies. It was an odd habit for a man who had just undergone a serious operation on his upper back, but, as he remarked to my mother one night, at least it gave him a world over which he had some control.

The family grew used to seeing him hunched down close to his tying vice, hackle pliers in one hand, thread bobbin in the other. We began to bandy about strange phrases – foxy quills, bodkins, peacock hurl. Father's corner of the living room was off limits to the maid with the voracious and destructive vacuum cleaner. Who knew what precious bit of calf's tail or rabbit fur would be sucked away never to be seen again.

Because of my father's illness, we had gone up to our summer cottage on the lake in New Hampshire a month early. None of my gang of friends ever came till the end of July, so in the beginning of that summer I hung around home watching my father as he fussed with the flies. I was the only child he allowed to stand near him while he worked. "Your brothers bounce," he muttered one day as he clamped the vice onto the curve of a model-perfect hook. "You can stay and watch if you don't bounce."

So I took great care not to bounce or lean or even breathe too noisily on him while he performed his delicate manoeuvres, holding back hackle with one hand as he pulled off the final flourish of a whip finish with the other. I had never been so close to my father for so long before, and while he studied his tiny creations, I studied him. I stared at the large pores of his skin, the sleek black hair brushed straight back from the soft dip of his temples, the jaw muscles tightening and slackening. Something in my father seemed always to be ticking. He did not take well to sickness and enforced confinement.

When he leaned over his work, his shirt collar slipped down to reveal the recent scar, a jagged trail of disrupted tissue. The tender pink skin gradually paled and then toughened during those weeks when he took his prescribed afternoon nap, lying on his stomach on our little patch of front lawn. Our house was one of the closest to the lake and it seemed to embarrass my mother to have him stretch himself out on the grass for all the swimmers and boaters to see.

"At least sleep on the porch," she would say. "That's why we set the hammock up there."

"Why shouldn't a man sleep on his own front lawn if he so chooses?" he would reply. "I have to mow the damn thing. I might as well put it to some use."

And my mother would shrug and give up.

At the table when he was absorbed, he lost all sense of anything but the magnified insect under the light. Often when he pushed his chair back and announced the completion of his latest project to the family, there would be a bit of down or a tuft of dubbing stuck to the edge of his lip. I did not tell him about it but stared, fascinated, wondering how long it would take to blow away. Sometimes it never did and I imagine he discovered the fluff in the bathroom mirror when he went upstairs to bed. Or maybe my mother plucked it off with one of those proprietary gestures of hers that irritated my brothers so much.

In the beginning, Father wasn't very good at the fly-tying. He was a large, thick-boned man with sweeping gestures, a robust laugh, and a sudden terrifying temper. If he had not loved fishing so much, I doubt he would have persevered with the fussy business of the flies. After all, the job required tools normally associated with woman's work. Thread and bobbins, soft slippery feathers, a magnifying glass, and an instruction manual that read like a cookbook. It said things like, "Cut off a bunch of yellowtail. Hold the tip end with the left hand and stroke out the short hairs."

But Father must have had a goal in mind. You tie flies because one day, in the not-too-distant future, you will attach them to a tippet, wade into a stream, and lure a rainbow trout out of his quiet pool.

There was something endearing, almost childish, about his stubborn nightly ritual at the corner table. His head bent under the standing lamp, his fingers trembling slightly, he would whisper encouragement to himself, talk his way through some particularly delicate operation. Once or twice I caught my mother gazing silently across my brothers' heads at him. When our eyes met, she would turn away and busy herself in the kitchen.

Finally, one night, after weeks of allowing me to watch, he told me to take his seat. "Why, Father?"

"Because it's time for you to try one."

"That's all right. I like to watch."

"Nonsense, Emily. You'll do just fine."

He had stood up. The chair was waiting. Across the room, my mother put down her knitting. Even the boys, embroiled in a noisy game of double solitaire, stopped their wrangling for a moment. They were all waiting to see what I would do. It was my fear of failing him that made me hesitate. I knew that my father put his trust in results, not in the learning process.

"Sit down, Emily."

I obeyed, my heart pounding. I was a cautious, secretive child, and I could not bear to have people watch me doing things. My piano lesson was the hardest hour in the week. The teacher would sit with a resigned look on her face while my fingers groped across the keys, muddling through a sonata that I had played perfectly just an hour before. The difference was that then nobody had been watching.

"—so we'll start you off with a big hook." He had been talking for some time. How much had I missed already?

"Ready?" he asked.

I nodded.

"All right then, clamp this hook into the vice. You'll be making the golden darter, a streamer. A big flashy fly, the kind that imitates a small fish as it moves underwater."

Across the room, my brothers had returned to their game, but their voices were subdued. I imagined they wanted to hear what was happening to me. My mother had left the room.

"Tilt the magnifying glass so you have a good view of the hook. Right. Now tie on with the bobbin thread."

It took me three tries to line the thread up properly on the hook, each silken line nesting next to its neighbour. "We're going to do it right, Emily, no matter how long it takes."

"It's hard," I said quietly.

Slowly I grew used to the tiny tools, to the oddly enlarged view of my fingers through the magnifying glass. They looked as if they didn't belong to me any more. The feeling in their tips was too small for their large, clumsy movements. Despite my father's repeated warnings, I nicked the floss once against the barbed hook. Luckily it did not give way.

"It's Emily's bedtime," my mother called from the kitchen.

"Hush, she's tying in the throat. Don't bother us now."

I could feel his breath on my neck. The mallard barbules were stubborn, curling into the hook in the wrong direction. Behind me, I sensed my father's fingers twisting in imitation of my own.

"You've almost got it," he whispered, his lips barely moving. "That's right. Keep the thread slack until you're all the way around."

I must have tightened it too quickly. I lost control of the feathers in my left hand, the clumsier one. First the gold mylar came unwound and then the yellow floss.

"Damn it all, now look what you've done," he roared, and for a second I wondered whether he was talking to me. He sounded as if he were talking to a grown-up. He sounded the way he had just the night before when an antique teacup had slipped through my mother's soapy fingers and shattered against the hard surface of the sink. I sat back slowly, resting my aching spine against the chair for the first time since we'd begun.

"Leave it for now, Gerald," my mother said tentatively from the kitchen. Out of the corner of my eye, I could see her sponging the kitchen counter with small, defiant sweeps of her hand. "She can try again tomorrow."

"What happened?" called a brother. They both started across the room towards us but stopped at a look from my father.

"We'll start again," he said, his voice once more under control. "Best way to learn. Get back on the horse."

With a flick of his hand, he loosened the vice, removed my hook, and threw it into the wastepaper basket.

"From the beginning?" I whispered.

"Of course," he replied. "There's no way to rescue a mess like that."

My mess had taken almost an hour to create.

"Gerald," my mother said again. "Don't you think—"

"How can we possibly work with all these interruptions?" he thundered. I flinched as if he had hit me. "Go on upstairs, all of you. Emily and I will be up when we're done. Go on, for God's sake. Stop staring at us."

At a signal from my mother, the boys backed slowly away and crept up to their room. She followed them. I felt all alone, as trapped under my father's piercing gaze as the hook in the grip of its vice.

We started again. This time my fingers were trembling so much that I ruined three badger hackle feathers, stripping off the useless webbing at the tip. My father did not lose his temper again. His voice dropped to an even, controlled monotone that scared me more than his shouting. After an hour of painstaking labour, we reached the same point with the stubborn mallard feathers curling into the hook. Once, twice, I repinched them under the throat, but each time they slipped away from me. Without a word, my father stood up and leaned over me. With his cheek pressed against my hair, he reached both hands around and took my fingers in his. I longed to surrender the tools to him and slide away off the chair, but we were so close to the end. He captured the curling stem with the thread and trapped it in place with three quick wraps.

"Take your hands away carefully," he said. "I'll do the whip finish. We don't want to risk losing it now."

I did as I was told, sat motionless with his arms around me, my head tilted slightly to the side so he could have the clear view through the magnifying glass. He cemented the head, wiped the excess glue from the eye with a waste feather, and hung my golden darter on the tackle box handle to dry. When at last he pulled away, I breathlessly slid my body back against the chair. I was still conscious of the havoc my clumsy hands or an unexpected sneeze could wreak on the table, which was cluttered with feathers and bits of fur.

"Now, that's the fly you tied, Emily. Isn't it beautiful?"

I nodded. "Yes, Father."

"Tomorrow, we'll do another one. An olive grouse. Smaller hook but much less complicated body. Look. I'll show you in the book."

As I waited to be released from the chair, I didn't think he meant it. He was just trying to apologize for having lost his temper, I told myself, just trying to pretend that our time together had been wonderful. But the next morning when I came down, late for breakfast, he was waiting for me with the materials for the olive grouse already assembled. He was ready to start in again, to take charge of my clumsy fingers with his voice and talk them through the steps.

That first time was the worst, but I never felt comfortable at the fly-tying table with Father's breath tickling the hair on my neck. I completed the olive grouse, another golden darter to match the first, two muddler minnows, and some others. I don't remember all the names any more.

Once I hid upstairs, pretending to be immersed in my summer reading books, but he came looking for me.

"Emily," he called. "Come on down. Today we'll start the lead-winged coachman. I've got everything set up for you."

I lay very still and did not answer.

"Gerald," I heard my mother say. "Leave the child alone. You're driving her crazy with those flies."

"Nonsense," he said, and started up the dark, wooden stairs, one heavy step at a time.

I put my book down and rolled slowly off the bed so that by the time he reached the door of my room, I was on my feet, ready to be led back downstairs to the table.

Although we never spoke about it, my mother became oddly insistent that I join her on trips to the library or the

227

general store.

"Are you going out again, Emily?" my father would call after me. "I was hoping we'd get some work done on this minnow."

"I'll be back soon, Father," I'd say. "I promise."

"Be sure you do," he said.

And for a while I did.

Then at the end of July, my old crowd of friends from across the lake began to gather and I slipped away to join them early in the morning before my father got up.

The girls were a gang. When we were all younger, we'd held bicycle relay races on the ring road and played down at the lake-side together under the watchful eyes of our mothers. Every July, we threw ourselves joyfully back into each other's lives. That summer we talked about boys and smoked illicit cigarettes in Randy Kidd's basement and held leg-shaving parties in her bedroom behind a safely locked door. Randy was the ringleader. She was the one who suggested we pierce our ears.

"My parents would die," I said. "They told me I'm not allowed to pierce my ears until I'm seventeen."

"Your hair's so long, they won't even notice," Randy said. "My sister will do it for us. She pierces all her friends' ears at college."

In the end, only one girl pulled out. The rest of us sat in a row with the obligatory ice cubes held to our ears, waiting for the painful stab of the sterilized needle.

Randy was right. At first my parents didn't notice. Even when my ears became infected, I didn't tell them. All alone in my room, I went through the painful procedure of twisting the gold studs and swabbing the recent wounds with alcohol. Then on the night of the club dance, when I had changed my clothes three times and played with my hair in front of the mirror for hours, I came across the small plastic box with dividers in my top bureau drawer. My father had given it to me so that I could keep my flies in separate compartments, untangled from one another. I poked my finger in and slid one of the golden darters up along its plastic wall. When I held it up, the mylar thread sparkled in the light like a jewel. I took out the other darter, hammered down the barbs of the two hooks, and slipped them into the raw holes in my earlobes.

Someone's mother drove us all to the dance, and Randy and I pushed through the side door into the ladies' room. I put my hair up in a ponytail so the feathered flies could twist and dangle above my shoulders. I liked the way they made me look – free and different and dangerous, even. And they made Randy notice.

"I've never seen ear-rings like that," Randy said. "Where did you get them?"

"I made them with my father. They're flies. You know, for fishing."

"They're great. Can you make me some?"

I hesitated. "I have some others at home I can give you," I said at last. "They're in a box in my bureau."

"Can you give them to me tomorrow?" she asked.

"Sure," I said with a smile. Randy had never noticed anything I'd worn before. I went out to the dance floor, swinging my ponytail in time to the music.

My mother noticed the ear-rings as soon as I got home.

"What has gotten into you, Emily? You know you were forbidden to pierce your ears until you were in college. This is appalling."

I didn't answer. My father was sitting in his chair behind the fly-tying table. His back was better by that time, but he still spent most of his waking hours in that chair. It was as if he didn't like to be too far away from his flies, as if something might blow away if he weren't keeping watch.

I saw him look up when my mother started in with me. His hands drifted ever so slowly down to the surface of the table as I came across the room towards him. I leaned over so that he could see my ear-rings better in the light.

"Everybody loved them, Father. Randy says she wants a pair, too. I'm going to give her the muddler minnows."

"I can't believe you did this, Emily," my mother said in a loud, nervous voice. "It makes you look so cheap."

"They don't make me look cheap, do they, Father?" I swung my head so he could see how they bounced, and my hip accidentally brushed the table. A bit of rabbit fur floated up from its pile and hung in the air for a moment before it settled down on top of the foxy quills.

"For God's sake, Gerald, speak to her," my mother said from her corner.

He stared at me for a long moment as if he didn't know who I was any more, as if I were a trusted associate who had committed some treacherous and unspeakable act.

"That is not the purpose for which the flies were intended," he said.

"Oh, I know that," I said quickly. "But they look good this way, don't they?"

He stood up and considered me in silence for a long time across the top of the table lamp.

"No, they don't," he finally said. "They're hanging upside down."

Then he turned off the light and I couldn't see his face any more.

GOAT'S TOBACCO

ROALD DAHL

from Boy – Tales of Childhood

WHEN I WAS ABOUT NINE, the ancient half-sister got engaged to be married. The man of her choice was a young English doctor and that summer he came with us to Norway. Romance was floating in the air like moondust and the two lovers, for some reason we younger ones could never understand, did not seem to be very keen on us tagging along with them. They went out in the boat alone. They climbed the rocks alone. They even had breakfast alone. We resented this. As a family we had always done everything together and we didn't see why the ancient half-sister should suddenly decide to do things differently even if she had become engaged. We were inclined to blame the male lover for disrupting the calm of our family life, and it was inevitable that he would have to suffer for it sooner or later.

The male lover was a great pipe-smoker. The disgusting smelly pipe was never out of his mouth except when he was eating or swimming. We even began to wonder whether he removed it when he was kissing his betrothed. He gripped the stem of the pipe in the most manly fashion between his strong white teeth and kept it there while talking to you. This annoyed us. Surely it was more polite to take it out and speak properly.

One day, we all went in our little motor-boat to an island we had never been to before, and for once the ancient half-sister and the manly lover decided to come with us. We chose this particular island because we saw some goats on it. They were climbing about on the rocks and we thought it would be fun to go and visit them. But when we landed, we found that the goats were totally wild and we couldn't get near them. So we gave up trying to make friends with them and simply sat around on the smooth rocks in our bathing costumes, enjoying the lovely sun.

The manly lover was filling his pipe. I happened to be watching him as he very carefully packed the tobacco into the bowl from a yellow oilskin pouch. He had just finished doing this and was about to light up when the ancient half-sister called on him to come swimming. So he put down the pipe and off he went.

I stared at the pipe that was lying there on the rocks. About twelve inches away from it, I saw a little heap of dried goat's droppings, each one small and round like a pale brown berry, and at that point, an interesting idea began to sprout in my mind. I picked up the pipe and knocked all the tobacco out of it. I then took the goat's droppings and teased them with my fingers until they were nicely shredded. Very gently I poured these shredded droppings into the bowl of the pipe, packing them down with my thumb just as the manly lover always did it. When that was done, I placed a thin layer of real tobacco over the top. The entire family was watching me as I did this. Nobody said a word, but I could sense a glow of approval all round. I replaced the pipe on the rock, and all of us sat back to await the return of the victim. The whole lot of us were in this together now, even my mother. I had drawn them into the plot simply by letting them see what I was doing. It was a silent, rather dangerous family conspiracy.

Back came the manly lover, dripping wet from the sea,

chest out, strong and virile, healthy and sunburnt. "Great swim!" he announced to the world. "Splendid water! Terrific stuff!" He towelled himself vigorously, making the muscles of his biceps ripple, then he sat down on the rocks and reached for his pipe.

Nine pairs of eyes watched him intently. Nobody giggled to give the game away. We were trembling with anticipation, and a good deal of the suspense was caused by the fact that none of us knew just what was going to happen.

The manly lover put the pipe between his strong white teeth and struck a match. He held the flame over the bowl and sucked. The tobacco ignited and glowed, and the lover's head was enveloped in clouds of blue smoke. "Ah-h-h," he said, blowing smoke through his nostrils. "There's nothing like a good pipe after a bracing swim."

Still we waited. We could hardly bear the suspense. The

sister who was seven couldn't bear it at all. "What *sort* of tobacco do you put in that thing?" she asked with superb innocence.

"Navy Cut," the male lover answered. "Player's Navy Cut. It's the best there is. These Norwegians use all sorts of disgusting scented tobaccos, but I wouldn't touch them."

"I didn't know they had different tastes," the small sister went on.

"Of course they do," the manly lover said. "All tobaccos are different to the discriminating pipe-smoker. Navy cut is clean and unadulterated. It's a man's smoke." The man seemed to go out of his way to use long words like discriminating and unadulterated. We hadn't the foggiest what they meant.

The ancient half-sister, fresh from her swim and now clothed in a towel bathrobe, came and sat herself close to her manly lover. Then the two of them started giving each other those silly little glances and soppy smiles that made us all feel sick. They were far too occupied with one another to notice the awful tension that had settled over our group. They didn't even notice that every face in the crowd was turned towards them. They had sunk once again into their lovers' world where little children did not exist.

The sea was calm, the sun was shining and it was a beautiful day.

Then all of a sudden, the manly lover let out a piercing scream and his whole body shot four feet into the air. His pipe flew out of his mouth and went clattering over the rocks, and the second scream he gave was so shrill and loud that all the seagulls on the island rose up in alarm. His features were twisted like those of a person undergoing severe torture, and his skin had turned the colour of snow. He began spluttering and choking and spewing and hawking and acting generally like a man with some serious internal injury. He was completely speech-less.

We stared at him, enthralled.

The ancient half-sister, who must have thought she was about to lose her future husband for ever, was pawing at him and thumping him on the back and crying, "Darling! Darling! What's happening to you? Where does it hurt? Get the boat! Start the engine! We must rush him to a hospital quickly!" She seemed to have forgotten that there wasn't a hospital within fifty miles.

"I've been poisoned!" spluttered the manly lover. "It's got into my lungs! It's in my chest! My chest is on fire! My stomach's going up in flames!"

"Help me get him into the boat! Quick!" cried the ancient half-sister, gripping him under the armpits. "Don't just sit there staring! Come and help!"

"No, no, no!" cried the now not-so-manly lover. "Leave me alone! I need air! Give me air!" He lay back and breathed in deep draughts of splendid Norwegian ocean air, and in another minute or so, he was sitting up again and was on the way to recovery.

"What in the world came over you?" asked the ancient half-sister, clasping his hands tenderly in hers.

"I can't imagine," he murmured. "I simply can't imagine." His face was as still and white as virgin snow and his hands were trembling. "There must be a reason for it," he added. "There's got to be a reason."

"I know the reason!" shouted the seven-year-old sister, screaming with laughter. "I know what it was!"

"What was it?" snapped the ancient one. "What have you been up to? Tell me at once!"

"It's his pipe!" shouted the small sister, still convulsed with laughter.

"What's wrong with my pipe?" said the manly lover.

"You've been smoking goat's tobacco!" cried the small sister.

It took a few moments for the full meaning of these words to dawn upon the two lovers, but when it did, and when the terrible anger began to show itself on the manly lover's face, and when he started to rise slowly and menacingly to his feet, we all sprang up and ran for our lives and jumped off the rocks into the deep water.

THE LADDER

V. S. PRITCHETT

"WE HAD THE BUILDERS in at the time," my father says in his accurate way, if he ever mentions his second marriage, the one that so quickly went wrong. "And," he says, clearing a small apology from his throat as though preparing to say something immodest, "we happened to be without stairs."

It is true. I remember that summer. I was fifteen years old. I came home from school at the end of the term, and when I got to our place not only had my mother gone but the stairs had gone too. There was no staircase in the house.

We lived in an old crab-coloured cottage, with long windows under the eaves that looked like eyes half-closed against the sun. Now when I got out of the car I saw scaffolding over the front door and two heaps of sand and mortar on the crazy paving, which my father asked me not to tread in because it would "make work for Janey." (This was the name of his second wife.) I went inside. Imagine my astonishment. The little hall had vanished, the ceiling had gone; you could see up to the roof; the wall on one

238

side had been stripped to the brick, and on the other hung a long curtain of builder's sheets. "Where are the stairs?" I said. "What have you done with the stairs?" I was at the laughing age.

A mild, trim voice spoke above our heads.

"Ah, I know that laugh," the voice said sweetly and archly. There was Miss Richards, or I should say my father's second wife, standing behind a builder's rope on what used to be the landing, which now stuck out precariously without banisters, like the portion of a ship's deck. The floor appeared to have been sawn off. She used to be my father's secretary and I had often seen her in my father's office; but now she had changed. Her fair hair was fluffed out and she wore a fussed and shiny brown dress that was quite unsuitable for the country.

I remember how odd they both looked, she up above and my father down below, and both apologizing to me. The builders had taken the old staircase out two days before, they said, and had promised to put the new one in against the far wall of the room behind the dust sheets before I got back from school. But they had not kept their promise.

"We go up," said my father, cutting his wife short, for she was apologizing too much, "by the ladder."

He pointed. At that moment his wife was stepping to the end of the landing where a short ladder, with a post to hold on to at the top as one stepped on the first rung, sloped eight or nine feet to the ground.

"It's horrible," called my step-mother.

My father and I watched her come down. She came to the post and turned round not sure whether she ought to come down the ladder frontwards or backwards.

"Back," called my father.

"No, the other hand on the post," he said.

My step-mother blushed fondly and gave him a look of fear. She put one foot on the step and then took her foot back and put the other one there and then pouted. It was only eight feet from the ground: at school we climbed half-way up the gym walls on the bars. I remembered her as a quick and practical woman at the office; she was now, I was sure, playing at being weak and dependent.

"My hands," she said, looking at the dust on her fingers as she grasped the top step.

My father and I stopped where we were and watched her. She put one leg out too high, as if, artlessly, to show the leg first. She was a plain woman and her legs (she used to say) were her "nicest thing". This was the only coquetry she had. She looked like one of those insects that try the air around them with their feelers before they move. I was surprised that my father (who had always been so polite and grave-mannered to my mother, and had almost bowed to me when he had met me at the station and helped me in and out of the car) did not go to help her. I saw an expression of obstinacy on his face.

"You're at the bottom," he said. "Only two more steps."

"Oh dear," said my step-mother, at last getting off the last step on to the floor; and she turned with her small chin raised, offering us her helplessness for admiration. She came to me and kissed me and said:

"Doesn't she look lovely? You are growing into a woman."

"Nonsense," said my father. And, in fear of being a woman, and yet pleased by what she said, I took my father's arm.

"Is that what we have to do? Is that how we get to bed?" I said.

"It's only until Monday," my father said again.

They both of them looked ashamed, as though by having the stairs removed they had done something foolish. My father tried to conceal this by an air of modest importance. They seemed a very modest couple. Both of them looked shorter to me since their marriage: I was very shocked by this. *She* seemed to have made him shorter. I had always thought of my father as a dark, vain, terse man, very

logical and never giving in to anyone. He seemed much
less important now his secretary was in the house.

"It is easy," I said, and I went to the ladder and was up
it in a moment.

"Mind," called my step-mother.

But in a moment I was down again, laughing. When I
was coming down I heard my step-mother say quietly to
my father, "What legs! She is growing."

My legs and my laugh: I did not think that my father's
secretary had the right to say anything about me. She was
not my mother.

After this my father took me round the house. I looked

behind me once or twice as I walked. On one of my shoes was some of the sand he had warned me about. I don't know how it got on my shoes. It was funny seeing this one sandy footmark making work for Janey wherever I went.

My father took me through the dust curtains into the dining-room and then to the far wall where the staircase was going to be.

"Why have you done it?" I said.

He and I were alone.

"The house has wanted it for years," he said. "It ought to have been done years ago."

I did not say anything. When my mother was here, she was always complaining about the house, saying it was poky, barbarous – I can hear her voice now saying "barbarous' as if it were the name of some terrifying and savage Queen – and my father had always refused to alter anything. Barbarous: I used to think of that word as my mother's name.

"Does Janey like it?" I said.

My father hardened at this question. He seemed to be saying, "What has it got to do with Janey?" But what he said was – and he spoke with amusement, with a look of quiet scorn:

"She liked it as it was."

"I did too," I said.

I then saw – but no, I did not really understand this at the time; it is something I understand now I am older – that my father was not altering the house for Janey's sake. She hated the whole place because my mother had been there, but was too tired by her earlier life in his office, fifteen years of it, too unsure of herself, to say anything. My father was making an act of amends to my mother. He was punishing Janey by "getting in builders" and making everyone uncomfortable and miserable; he was making an emotional scene with himself. He was annoying Janey with what my mother had so maddeningly wanted and which he would not give her.

After he had shown me the house, I said I would go and see Janey getting lunch ready.

"I shouldn't do that," said my father. "It will delay her. Lunch is just ready.

"Or should be," he said, looking at his watch.

We went to the sitting-room, and while we waited I sat in the green chair and he asked me questions about school and we went on to talk about the holidays. But when I answered I could see he was not listening to me but trying to catch sounds of Janey moving in the kitchen. Occasionally there were sounds: something gave an explosive fizz in a hot pan, and a saucepan lid fell. This made a loud noise and the lid spun a long time on the stone floor. The sound stopped our talk.

"Janey is not used to the kitchen," said my father.

I smiled very close to my lips, I did not want my father to see it, but he looked at me and he smiled by accident too. There was understanding between us.

"I will go and see," I said.

He raised his hand to stop me, but I went.

It was natural. For fifteen years Janey had been my father's secretary. She had worked in an office. I remember when I went there when I was young she used to come into the room with an earnest air, leaning her head a little sideways and turning three-quarter-face to my father at his desk, leaning forward to guess at what he wanted. I admired the great knowledge she had of his affairs, the way she carried letters, how quickly she picked up the telephone if it rang, the authority of her voice. Her strength was that she had been impersonal. She had lost that strength in her marriage. As his wife, she had no behaviour. When we were talking she raised her low bosom, which had become round and duck-like, with a sigh and smiled at my father with a tentative, expectant fondness. After fifteen years, a life had ended: she was resting.

But Janey had not lost her office behaviour: that she now

kept for the kitchen. The moment I went to the kitchen, I saw her walking to the stove where the saucepans were throbbing too hard. She was walking exactly as she had walked towards my father at his desk. The stove had taken my father's place. She went up to it with impersonal enquiry, as if to anticipate what it wanted, she appeared to be offering a pile of plates to be warmed as if they were a pile of letters. She seemed baffled because the stove could not speak. When one of the saucepans boiled over she ran to it and lifted it off, suddenly and too high, with her telephone movement: the water spilled at once. On the table beside the stove were basins and pans she was using, and she had them all spread out in an orderly way like typing; she went from one to the other with the careful look of enquiry she used to give to the things she was filing. It was not a method suitable to work in a kitchen.

When I came in, she put down the pan she was holding and stopped everything – as she would have done in the office – to talk to me about what she was doing. She was very nice about my hair, which I had had cut last term; it made me look older and I liked it better. But blue smoke rose behind her as we talked. She did not notice it.

I went back to my father.

"I didn't want to be in the way," I said.

"Extraordinary," he said, looking at his watch. "I must just go and hurry Janey up."

He was astonished that a woman so brisk in an office should be languid and dependent in a house.

"She is just bringing it in," I said. "The potatoes are ready. They are on the table. I saw them."

"On the table?" he said. "Getting cold?"

"On the kitchen table," I said.

"That doesn't prevent them being cold," he said. My father was a sarcastic man.

I walked about the room humming. My father's exasperation did not last; it gave way to a new thing in his voice. Resignation.

"We will wait if you do not mind," he said to me. "Janey is slow. And by the way," he said, lowering his voice a little, "I shouldn't mention we passed the Leonards in the road when I brought you up from the station."

I was surprised.

"Not the Leonards?" I said.

"They were friends of your mother's," he said. "You are old enough to understand. One has to be sometimes a little tactful. Janey sometimes feels . . ."

I looked at my father. He had altered in many ways. When he gave me this secret his small, brown eyes gave a brilliant flash and I opened my blue eyes very wide to receive it. He had changed. His rough black hair was clipped closer at the ears and he had that too young look which middle-aged men sometimes have, for by certain lines it can be seen that they are not as young as their faces. Marks like the minutes on the face of a clock showed at the corners of his eyes, his nose, his mouth; he was much thinner; his face had hardened. He had often been angry and sarcastic, sulking and abrupt, when my mother was with us; I had never seen him before, as he was now, blank-faced, ironical and set in impatient boredom. After he spoke, he had actually been hissing a tune privately through his teeth at the corner of his mouth. At this moment Janey came in with a smile but without dishes, and said lunch was ready.

"Oh," I laughed when we got into the dining-room. "It is like . . . it is like France."

"France?" they both said together, smiling at me.

"Like when we all went to France before the war and you took the car," I said. I had chosen France because that seemed as far as I could get from the Leonards.

"What on earth are you talking about?" said my father, looking embarrassed. "You were only five before the war."

"I remember every bit of it. You and Mummy on the boat."

"Yes, yes," said my step-mother with melancholy importance. "I got the tickets for you all."

My father looked as though he was going to hit me. Then he gave a tolerant laugh across the table to my step-mother.

"I remember perfectly well," she said. "I'm afraid I couldn't get the peas to boil. Oh, I've forgotten the potatoes."

"Fetch them," my father said to me.

I thought she was going to cry. When I came back, I could see she *had* been crying. She was one of those very fair women in whom even three or four tears bring pink to the nose. My father had said something sharply to her, for his face was shut and hard and she was leaning over the dishes, a spoon in her hand, to conceal a wound.

After lunch I took my case and went up the ladder. It was not easy to go up carrying a suitcase, but I enjoyed it. I wished we could always have a ladder in the house. It was like being on a ship. I stood at the top thinking of my mother leaning on the rail of the ship with her new husband, going to America. I was glad she had gone because, sometimes, she sent me lovely things.

Then I went to my room and I unpacked my case. At the bottom, when I took my pyjamas out – they were the last thing – there was the photograph of my mother face downwards where it had been lying all the term. I forgot to say that I had been in trouble the last week at school. I don't know why. I was longing to be home. I felt I had to *do* something. One afternoon I went into the rooms in our passage when no one was there, and I put the snap of Kitty's father into Mary's room – I took it out of the frame – and I put Mary's brother into Olga's, and I took Maeve's mother and put her into the silver frame where Jessie's mother was: that photograph was too big and I bent the mount all the way down to get it in. Maeve cried and

reported me to Miss Compton. "It was only a joke," I said. "A joke in very poor taste," Miss Compton said to me in *her* voice. "How would you like it if anyone took the photograph of your mother?" "I haven't got one," I said. Well, it was not a lie. Everyone wanted to know why I had an empty frame on my chest of drawers. I had punished my mother by leaving her photograph in my trunk.

But now the punishment was over. I took out her picture and put it in the frame on my chest, and every time I bent up from the drawers I looked at her, then at myself in the mirror. In the middle of this my step-mother came in to ask if she could help me.

"You are getting very pretty," she said. I hated her for admiring me.

I do not deny it: I hated her. She was a foolish woman. She either behaved as if the house, my father and myself were too much hers, or as if she were an outsider. Most of the time she sat there like a visitor, waiting for attention.

I thought to myself: There is my mother, thousands of miles away, leaving us to this and treating us like dirt, and we are left with Miss Richards, of all people.

That night after I had gone to bed I heard my father and my step-mother having a quarrel. "It is perfectly natural," I heard my father say, "for the child to have a photograph of her mother."

A door closed. Someone was wandering about in the passage. When they had gone I opened my door and crept out barefoot to listen. Every step I made seemed to start a loud creak in the boards and I was so concerned with this that I did not notice I had walked to the edge of the landing. The rope was there, but in the dark I could not see it. I knew I was on the edge of the drop into the hall and that with one more step I would have gone through. I went back to my room, feeling sick. And then the thought struck me – and I could not get it out of my head all night; I dreamed it, I tried not to dream it, I turned on the light, but I dreamed it again – that Miss Richards fell over the edge of the landing. I was very glad when the morning came.

The moment I was downstairs I laughed at myself. The drop was only eight or nine feet. Anyone could jump it. I worked out how I would land on my feet if I were to jump there. I moved the ladder, it was not heavy to lift, to see what you would feel like if there were no ladder there and the house was on fire and you had to jump. To make amends for my wicked dreams in the night I saw myself rescuing Miss Richards (I should say my step-mother) as flames teased her to the edge.

My father came out of his room and saw me standing there.

"What are you pulling such faces for?" he said. And he imitated my expressions.

"I was thinking," I said, "of Miss Compton at our school."

He had not foreseen the change in Miss Richards; how she would sit in the house in her best clothes, like a visitor, expectant, forgetful, stunned by leisure, watchful, wronged and jealous to the point of tears.

Perhaps if the builders had come, as they had promised, on the Monday, my step-mother's story would have been different.

"I am so sorry we are in such a mess," she said to me many times, as if she thought I regarded the ladder as her failure.

"It's fun," I said. "It's like being on a ship."

"You keep on saying that," my step-mother said, looking at me in a very worried way, as if trying to work out the hidden meaning of my remark. "You've never been on a ship."

"To France," I said. "When I was a child."

"Oh yes, you told me," said my step-mother.

Life had become so dull for my father that he liked having the ladder in the house.

"I hate it," said my step-mother to both of us, getting

up. It is always surprising when a prosaic person becomes angry.

"Do leave us alone," my father said.

There was a small scene after this. My father did not mean by "us" himself and me, as she chose to think; he was simply speaking of himself, and he had spoken very mildly. My step-mother marched out of the room. Presently we heard her upstairs. She must have been very upset to have faced going up the ladder.

"Come on," said my father. "I suppose there's nothing for it. I'll get the car out. We will go the builder's."

He called up to her that we were going.

Oh, it was a terrible holiday. When I grew up and was myself married, my father said: "It was a very difficult summer. You didn't realize. You were only a schoolgirl. It was a mistake." And then he corrected himself. I mean that: my father was always making himself more correct: it was his chief vanity that he understood his own behaviour.

"I happened," he said – this was the correction – "to make a very foolish mistake." Whenever he used the phrase "I happened" my father's face seemed to dry up and become distant: he was congratulating himself. Not on the mistake, of course, but on being the first to put his finger on it. "I happen to know . . . I happen to have seen . . ." – it was this incidental rightness, the footnote of inside knowledge on innumerable minor issues, and his fatal wrongness in a large, obstinate, principled way about anything important, which, I think, made my beautiful and dishonest mother leave him. She was a tall woman, taller than he, with the eyes of a cat, shrugging her shoulders, curving her long graceful back to be stroked and with a wide, champagne laugh. My father had a clipped-back monkeyish appearance and that faint grin of the bounder one sees in the harder-looking monkeys that are without melancholy or sensibility; this had attracted my mother, but very soon his youthful bounce gave place to a kind of meddling honesty, and she found him dull. And, of course, ruthless. The promptness of his second marriage, perhaps, was to teach her a lesson. I imagine him putting his divorce papers away one evening at his office and realizing, when Miss Richards came in to ask if "there is anything more tonight," that there was a woman who was reliable, trained and, like himself, "happened" to have a lot of inside knowledge.

To get out of the house with my father, to be alone with him: my heart came alive. It seemed to me that this house was not my home any more. If only we could go away, he and I; the country outside seemed to me far more like home than this grotesque divorced house. I stood longing for my step-mother not to answer, dreading that she would come down.

My father was not a man to beg a woman to change her mind. He went out to the garage. My fear of her coming made me stay for a moment. And then (I do not know how the thought came into my head) I went to the ladder and I lifted it away. It was easy to move a short distance, but it began to swing when I tried to put it down. I was afraid it would crash, so I turned it over and over against the other wall, out of reach. Breathlessly, I left the house.

"You have got white on your tunic," said my father as we drove off. "What have you been doing?"

"I rubbed against something," I said.

"Oh, how I love motoring," I laughed beside my father.

"Oh, look at those lovely little rabbits," I said.

"Their little white tails," I laughed.

We passed some hurdles in a field.

"Jumps," I laughed. "I wish I had a pony."

And then my terrible dreams came back to me. I was frightened. I tried to think of something else, but I could not. I could only see my step-mother on the edge of the landing. I could only hear her giving a scream and going over head first. We got into the town and I felt sick. We arrived at the builder's and my father stopped there. Only a girl was in the office, and I heard my father say in his

251

coldest voice, "I happen to have an appointment . . ."

My father came out, and we drove off. He was cross.

"Where are we going?" I said, when I saw we were not going home.

"To Longwood," he said. "They're working over there." I thought I would faint.

"I – I . . . " I began.

"What?" my father said.

I could not speak. I began to get red and hot. And then I remembered. "I can pray."

It is seven miles to Longwood. My father was a man who enjoyed talking to builders; he planned and replanned with them, built imaginary houses, talked about people. Builders have a large acquaintance with the way people live; my father liked inside knowledge, as I have said. Well, I thought, she is over. She is dead by now. I saw visits to the hospital. I saw my trial.

"She is like you," said the builder, nodding to me. All my life I shall remember his moustache. ·

"She is like my wife," said my father. "My first wife. I happen to have married again."

(He liked puzzling and embarrassing people.)

"Do you happen to know a tea place near here?" he said.

"Oh no," I said. "I don't feel hungry."

But we had tea at Gilling. The river is across the road from the tea-shop and we stood afterwards on the bridge. I surprised my father by climbing the parapet.

"If you jumped," I said to my father, "would you hurt?"

"You'd break your legs," said my father.

Her "nicest thing"!

I shall not describe our drive back to the house, but my father did say, "Janey will be worried. We've been nearly three hours. I'll put the car in afterwards."

When we got back, he got out quickly and went down the path. I got out slowly. It is a long path leading across a small lawn, then between two lime trees; there are a few steps down where the roses are, and across another piece of grass you are at the door. I stopped to listen to the bees in the limes, but I could not wait any longer. I went into the house.

There was my step-mother standing on the landing above the hall. Her face was dark red, her eyes were long and violent, her dress was dirty and her hands were black with dust. She had just finished screaming something at my father and her mouth had stayed open after her scream. I thought I could *smell* her anger and her fear the moment I came into the house, but it was really the smell of a burned-out saucepan coming from the kitchen.

"You moved the ladder! Six hours I've been up here. The telephone has been ringing, something has burned on the stove. I might have burned to death. Get me down, get me down. I might have killed myself. Get me down," she cried, and she came to the gap where the ladder ought to have been.

"Don't be silly, Janey," said my father. "I didn't move the ladder. Don't be such a fool. You're still alive."

"Get me down," Janey cried out. "You liar, you liar, you liar. You did move it."

My father lifted the ladder, and as he did so he said:

"The builder must have been."

"No one has been," screamed my step-mother. "I've been alone. Up here!"

"Daddy isn't a liar," I said, taking my father's arm.

"Come down," said my father when he had got the ladder in place. "I'm holding it."

And he went up a step or two towards her.

"No," shrieked Janey, coming to the edge.

"Now, come on. Calm yourself," said my father.

"No, no, I tell you," said Janey.

"All right, you must stay," said my father, and stepped down.

That brought her, of course.

"*I* moved the ladder," I said when she came down.

"Oh," said Janey, swinging her arm to hit me, but she fainted instead.

That night my father came to my room when I was in bed. I had moved my mother's photograph to the bedside table. He was not angry. He was tired out.

"Why did you do it?" he asked.

I did not answer.

"Did you know she was upstairs?" he said.

I did not reply.

"Stop playing with the sheet," he said. "Look at me. Did you know she was upstairs?"

"Yes," I said.

"You little cat," he said.

I smiled.

"It was very wrong," he said.

I smiled. Presently he smiled. I laughed.

"It is nothing to laugh at," he said. And suddenly he could not stop himself: he laughed. The door opened and my step-mother looked in while we were both shaking with laughter. My father laughed as if he were laughing for the first time for many years; his bounderish look, sly and bumptious and so delicious, came back to him. The door closed.

He stopped laughing.

"She might have been killed," he said, severely again.

"No, no, no," I cried, and tears came to my eyes.

He put his arm round me.

My mother was a cat, they said, a wicked woman, leaving us like that. I longed for my mother.

Three days later, I went camping. I apologized to my step-mother and she forgave me. I never saw her again.

Acknowledgements

The publisher would like to thank the copyright holders for permission to reproduce the following copyright material:

Nina Bawden: Penguin Books Ltd for Chapter 2 from *Carrie's War* by Nina Bawden. Copyright © 1973 by Nina Bawden. Published in Penguin Books 1974. **Judy Blume**: Random House UK Ltd for "The TV Star" from *Tales of a Fourth Grade Nothing* by Judy Blume (Bodley Head 1979). Copyright © 1972 by Judy Blume. **Betsy Byars**: Scholastic Inc for "Sam's Storm" by Betsy Byars from *In Another World and Other Stories* (Scholastic Inc 1985). **Ann Cameron**: Victor Gollancz Ltd for "Catalogue Cats" from *The Julian Stories* by Ann Cameron. Copyright © 1981 by Ann Cameron. **Robert Cormier**: HarperCollins Publishers Ltd for "President Cleveland, Where Are You?" from *Eight Plus One: Stories by Robert Cormier*. Copyright © by Robert Cormier. **Roald Dahl**: Murray Pollinger for "Goat's Tobacco" from *Boy – Tales of Childhood* by Roald Dahl (Jonathan Cape Ltd and Penguin Books Ltd). Copyright © 1984 by Roald Dahl. **Jane Gardam**: Penguin Books Ltd for the extract from *Bilgewater* by Jane Gardam. Copyright © 1976 by Jane Gardam. First published by Hamish Hamilton Books 1976. **Graham Greene**: David Higham Associates for "I Spy" from *Collected Stories of Graham Greene* by Graham Greene. Copyright © 1972 by Graham Greene (Heinemann). **Laurence Lasky**: Scholastic Inc for "The Cement Truck" by Laurence Lasky from *Discovery* (Scholastic Book Services 1967). **Jean Little**: Penguin Books Canada Ltd for the extract from *Little by Little* by Jean Little. Copyright © 1987 by Jean Little. **Kevin Major**: Dell Books, a division of Bantam Doubleday Dell Publishing Group Inc and Sterling Lord Associates (Canada) Ltd for the extract from *Dear Bruce Springsteen*. Copyright © 1987 by Kevin Major. **Richard Parker**: Kathleen Parker for "Lion By Moonlight" from *Lion at Large* by Richard Parker (Nelson 1961). Copyright © 1961 by Richard Parker. **Philippa Pearce**: Philippa Pearce and Laura Cecil Literary Agency for "Who's Afraid?" from *Who's Afraid? and Other Strange Stories* by Philippa Pearce. Copyright © 1978 by Philippa Pearce (Viking Kestrel). **V.S. Pritchett**: Random House UK Ltd for "The Ladder" from *More Collected Stories* by V.S. Pritchett (Chatto & Windus). Copyright © 1955 by V.S. Pritchett. **Lynne Reid Banks**: Vallentine Mitchell & Company Ltd for the extract from *One More River* by Lynne Reid Banks, copyright © by Vallentine Mitchell & Co Ltd. **Cynthia Rylant**: Bradbury Press, Macmillan Publishing for "Stray" from *Every Living Thing*. Copyright © 1985 by Cynthia Rylant. **William Saroyan**: Laurence Pollinger Ltd and the William Saroyan Foundation for "The Stolen Bicycle" from *Dear Baby*. Copyright © by William Saroyan. **John Steinbeck**: Reed Consumer Books for the extract from *The Red Pony* by John Steinbeck (Heinemann). Copyright © 1938 by John Steinbeck. **Sue Townsend**: Reed Consumer Books for the extract from *The Secret Diary of Adrian Mole, Aged 13¾* by Sue Townsend (Methuen). Copyright © 1982 by Sue Townsend. **Ethel Turner**: Philippa Poole for "The General Sees Active Service" from *Seven Little Australians* (Angus & Robertson). Copyright © 1894 by Ethel Turner. **Marjorie Weinman Sharmat**: Marjorie Sharmat for "May I Have Your Autograph?" by Marjorie Weinman Sharmat. Copyright © 1984 by Marjorie Sharmat. **Jessamyn West**: Russell & Volkering as agents for the author for "Reverdy" from *Collected Stories of Jessamyn West*. Copyright © 1986 by Harry Maxwell McPherson. **Elizabeth Winthrop**: Elizabeth Winthrop for "The Golden Darters" first published in *American Short Fiction*. Copyright © 1991 by Elizabeth Winthrop. **Paul Zindel**: Random House UK Ltd for the extract from *The Pigman and Me* by Paul Zindel (Bodley Head 1991). Copyright © 1991 by Paul Zindel.

Every effort has been made to obtain permission to reproduce copyright material but there may be cases where we have been unable to trace a copyright holder. The publisher will be happy to correct any omissions in future printings.